An OVID Workbook

Latin Literature Workbook Series

A Series Edited by LeaAnn A. Osburn

A Horace Workbook (2005)

A Horace Workbook Teacher's Manual (2006)

A Vergil Workbook (2006)

A Vergil Workbook Teacher's Manual (2007)

An Ovid Workbook (2006)

An Ovid Workbook Teacher's Manual (2007)

A Catullus Workbook (2006)

A Catullus Workbook Teacher's Manual (2007)

A Cicero Workbook (2006)

A Cicero Workbook Teacher's Manual (2007)

An OVID Workbook

Charbra Adams Jestin
& Phyllis B. Katz

Bolchazy-Carducci Publishers, Inc.
Wauconda, Illinois USA

Series Editor
LeaAnn A. Osburn

Volume General Editor
Donald E. Sprague

Typography, Page and Cover Design
Adam Phillip Velez

An Ovid Workbook

by Charbra Adams Jestin & Phyllis B. Katz

© 2006 Bolchazy-Carducci Publishers, Inc.
All rights reserved.

Bolchazy-Carducci Publishers, Inc.
1000 Brown Street
Wauconda, IL 60084 USA
www.bolchazy.com

Printed in the United States of America
2007
by United Graphics

ISBN 978-0-86516-625-7

CONTENTS

Foreword vii

Preface ix

Text of the *Amores* with Exercises 1
    Amores 1.1. 2
    Amores 1.3 8
    Amores 1.9. 14
    Amores 1.11 22
    Amores 1.12 30
    Amores 3.15 38

Text Selections from the *Metamorphoses* with Exercises 45
    Apollo and Daphne
        1.452–487 46
        1.488–524 52
        1.525–567 58
    Pyramus and Thisbe
        4.55–92 66
        4.93–127. 72
        4.128–166 78
    Daedalus and Icarus
        8.183–235 86
    Philemon and Baucis
        8.616–650 94
        8.651–678 100
        8.679–724 106

Pygmalion
- 10.238–266 114
- 10.267–297 120

Appendices A and B 127
- Appendix A: Practice Exams 128
- Appendix B: High Frequency Word List 137

A Complete Vocabulary 139

FOREWORD

All Latin teachers want their students to read ancient authors in the original. Yet to study the authentic Latin of an ancient Roman author is a complex task. It requires comprehension of the text and its grammatical underpinnings; an understanding of the world events and the culture in which the work of literature was produced; an ability to recognize the figures of speech the author uses and to grasp the impact they have on the text; sensitivity to the way sound effects, including meter if a passage is poetry, interact with the meaning of the text; and the ability to probe whatever thoughts and ideas the author may be expressing. To be successful in this multifaceted task, students need not only a comprehensive textbook but also exercises of different kinds, in which to practice their newly developing literary and critical skills.

Students often need extensive drill and practice material—something not available in the traditional Latin author textbook—to help them master the grammar and syntax of the Latin text as well as the literary skills that the text demands of its readers. Teachers, too, no matter how many questions they ask in class to help their students analyze the syntax and the literary qualities of the text, often need and want more questions to be available. Realizing this need on the part of both students and teachers, Bolchazy-Carducci Publishers has begun to develop a series of workbooks to accompany Advanced Placement textbooks. There will be five workbooks in the series, one for each advanced placement author: Catullus, Cicero, Horace, Ovid, and Vergil. A team of authors—one, a university scholar with special expertise in the Latin literary text and the other, a high school Advanced Placement Latin teacher—will write each workbook.

Workbooks in this series will contain the Latin text as delineated on the Advanced Placement Syllabus and exercises that drill grammar, syntax, and figures of speech. In addition, multiple choice questions will be included and will focus on the student's comprehension of the passage and on items of literary analysis. The workbooks will also feature scansion practice, essays to write, and other short analysis questions in each section. By reading and answering these types of questions, students will gain experience with the types of questions that are found on the Advanced Placement Examinations.[*] Students at the college level will also benefit from the additional practice offered in the workbooks.

These workbooks contain neither textual notes nor vocabulary on the page with the text nor on the facing page. The absence of these traditional features of textbooks will allow students, after reading the Latin passage in the textbook, to practice in the workbook what they have learned and to assess how much they have mastered already and what needs more study. The workbooks will, however, contain a Latin to English Vocabulary at the back of the book.

We are confident that this series of workbooks has a unique role to play in fostering students' understanding of authentic Latin text and will be a significant addition to the Advanced Placement and college materials that already exist.

LeaAnn A. Osburn
Series Editor

---

[*] AP is a registered trademark of the College Entrance Examination Board, which was not involved in the production of, and does not endorse, this product.

PREFACE

This workbook has been designed to give students confidence in reading the poetry of Ovid with full comprehension. Students preparing for the nationally-administered Advanced Placement Latin Literature Exam in Ovid will find ample practice for that exam in this workbook. College students using this workbook will find a useful resource for their study of Ovid's poetry. The workbook can be used in conjunction with any edition of Ovid's poems. The text printed and the Latin Vocabulary included are those published in our text, *Ovid: Amores, Metamorphoses, Selections* (Wauconda, IL: Bolchazy-Carducci Publishers, 1998, Second edition, 2003).

You will find several types of questions in each chapter to help strengthen students' ability to understand the composition of Ovid's poetry and its meaning. The first part of each chapter contains questions targeting grammatical analysis of the passage at hand. Questions of this sort help to confirm that students are reading the Latin of the passage accurately.

Each chapter of the workbook also includes a second part with multiple choice questions. These test a variety of material in the passage: structure, translation, comprehension, figures of speech, scansion, and references. We have included these in this workbook as a means for students to practice and evaluate their skills in these areas. The figure of speech that is sometimes called interlocked word order is identified in this workbook by the more formal term "synchesis," which is also spelled "synchysis" in some texts. Tricolon crescendo, sometimes called tricolon crescens in other texts, is the term used in this workbook.

In the third part of each chapter in this workbook students will gain practice in rendering into literal English a six- to eight-line segment from the passage in the chapter. This exercise represents the same length selection as on the Advanced Placement exam. Students should strive for the greatest accuracy possible in the translation of these selections, and should bear in mind that accurate translation is an aid to reading Latin with fluency.

Each chapter also includes a fourth part with short response questions of the sort seen in the Identification Questions on the Advanced Placement exam or comparable college Latin exams. The questions are generally worded to lead the student to a short, rather specific answer.

For each of the *Amores* and each of the longer passages from the *Metamorphoses* you will also find a section that contains a twenty-minute essay topic. These essays should be written on a separate sheet of paper. The more practice students have in writing these essays the better they become at writing concise, yet strong essays that are based specifically on the question posed. In each essay students should provide ample reference to the Latin, properly cited, either translated or paraphrased accurately, that supports their argument. Essays should always be analytical in nature rather than a narrative, that is, students should not summarize a passage but rather construct an argument that is based on the Latin that applies to the essay question.

---

* AP is a registered trademark of the College Entrance Examination Board, which was not involved in the production of, and does not endorse, this product.

You will also find a part that gives students practice in scanning lines from the passages. *Scansion should always be a part of poetic analysis* and may add weight to an argument made in an essay.

A final supplementary part asks students to work with the vocabulary of the passage. Vocabulary building is an important part of students' preparation for reading Ovid confidently. Without a sufficient vocabulary, students stumble through translations and give weak answers. Some of the vocabulary sections ask students to search for words with a common theme, while other sections ask them to recall words and to learn words that they do not yet know. As students gain more familiarity with Ovid's vocabulary, they will understand and appreciate his poetry more fully.

Over the course of their study of the passages from the *Amores* and the *Metamorphoses,* students will be reading some wonderful literature and will come to understand the poetic voice Ovid has created for himself in his poems. We are certain that with diligence and with the help of the exercises in this workbook, students will expand and enhance their ability to enjoy and admire this author's poetry.

CHARBRA ADAMS JESTIN
Avon High School
Avon, Connecticut

PHYLLIS B. KATZ
Dartmouth College
Hanover, New Hampshire

TEXT OF
THE *AMORES*
WITH EXERCISES

AMORES 1.1

    Arma gravi numero violentaque bella parabam
        edere, materia conveniente modis.
    par erat inferior versus; risisse Cupido
        dicitur atque unum surripuisse pedem.
5   "quis tibi, saeve puer, dedit hoc in carmina iuris?
        Pieridum vates, non tua, turba sumus.
    quid si praeripiat flavae Venus arma Minervae,
        ventilet accensas flava Minerva faces?
    quis probet in silvis Cererem regnare iugosis,
10   lege pharetratae virginis arva coli?
    crinibus insignem quis acuta cuspide Phoebum
        instruat, Aoniam Marte movente lyram?
    sunt tibi magna, puer, nimiumque potentia regna:
        cur opus affectas ambitiose novum?
15   an, quod ubique, tuum est? tua sunt Heliconia tempe?
        vix etiam Phoebo iam lyra tuta sua est?
    cum bene surrexit versu nova pagina primo,
        attenuat nervos proximus ille meos.
    nec mihi materia est numeris levioribus apta,
20   aut puer aut longas compta puella comas."
    questus eram, pharetra cum protinus ille soluta
        legit in exitium spicula facta meum
    lunavitque genu sinuosum fortiter arcum
        "quod" que "canas, vates, accipe" dixit "opus."
25   me miserum! certas habuit puer ille sagittas.
        uror, et in vacuo pectore regnat Amor.
    sex mihi surgat opus numeris, in quinque residat;
        ferrea cum vestris bella valete modis.
    cingere litorea flaventia tempora myrto,
30   Musa per undenos emodulanda pedes.

Short Answer Questions

Line 1   What is the case and use of *arma* and *bella*? _____

Line 2   What is the case and use of *materia conveniente*? _____

Line 7   What is the tense and mood of *praeripiat*? _____

             What is the reason for that tense and mood? _____

Line 9   What are the tense, mood, and voice of *regnare*? _____

                What is the reason for that mood? _____

                What is the case and use of *Cererem*? _____

Line 11   What is the case and use of *crinibus*? _____

Line 13   What is the case and use of *tibi*? _____

Line 24   What is the tense and mood of *canas*? _____

                What is the reason for that tense and mood? _____

Line 25   What is the case and use of *me miserum*? _____

Line 29   What is the tense and mood of *cingere*? _____

                What is the reason for that tense and mood? _____

Multiple Choice Questions *Suggested time: 12 minutes*

1. The examples cited in lines 7–12 are to suggest
   a. that the gods cannot have their roles reversed
   b. that there is rivalry among the gods
   c. the reasons that Cupid and the poet are not alike
   d. that Cupid is ambitious

2. A figure of speech found in lines 7–12 is
   a. hyperbaton
   b. polysyndeton
   c. tricolon crescendo
   d. onomatopoeia

3. In line 8, the poet uses the figure of speech
   a. litotes
   b. personification
   c. metaphor
   d. chiasmus

4. In line 8, the *faces* refer to
   a. anger
   b. torch light
   c. love and marriage
   d. rods of authority

5. The metrical pattern for the first four feet of line 19 is
   a. dactyl-spondee-dactyl-dactyl
   b. dactyl-dactyl-dactyl-dactyl
   c. spondee-spondee-dactyl-spondee
   d. dactyl-dactyl-spondee-dactyl

6. The case of *longas comas* (line 20) is governed by
   a. *puella*
   b. *materia*
   c. *puer*
   d. *compta*

7. In line 21, the case and number of *pharetra* are
   a. nominative singular
   b. nominative plural
   c. ablative singular
   d. accusative plural

8. In lines 19–20, the poet tells us
   a. that he is not in love
   b. that he has a girl friend
   c. that he has a boy friend
   d. that he is unhappy

9. Lines 27–28 tell us that
   a. the poet will continue to write epic poetry
   b. the poet cannot write elegiac (love) poetry
   c. the poet will now write elegiac poetry
   d. love poetry is full of harsh wars

10. In line 30, the case and number of *emodulanda* are
    a. ablative singular
    b. nominative plural
    c. vocative singular
    d. nominative singular

Translation *Suggested time: 15 minutes*

Translate the passage below as literally as possible.

sunt tibi magna, puer, nimiumque potentia regna:
    cur opus affectas ambitiose novum?
an, quod ubique, tuum est? tua sunt Heliconia tempe?
    vix etiam Phoebo iam lyra tuta sua est?
5   cum bene surrexit versu nova pagina primo,
    attenuat nervos proximus ille meos.
nec mihi materia est numeris levioribus apta,
    aut puer aut longas compta puella comas.

Short Analysis Questions

1. a. Translate *saeve puer* (line 5). _____

   b. When the poet calls Cupid *"saeve"* here, what figure of speech is he employing?
   _____

2. In lines 13–14, the poet describes Cupid's sphere of influence.

   a. What figure of speech does he employ here?
   _____

   b. Write out the exact Latin words that express the figure of speech.
   _____

3. a. Exactly what is the poet describing in lines 17–18?
   _____

   b. Write out a literal translation for these lines.
   _____
   _____
   _____

4. a. To what muse does the poet refer in lines 29–30? _____

   b. Write out and translate the Latin words that help to identify this muse.
   _____
   _____

Essay *Suggested time: 20 minutes*

In *Amores* 1.1, the poet describes himself as tricked and/or forced by Cupid to renounce the writing of epic poetry and instead become a love poet. Write an essay in which you discuss the nature of the love god's trick and the poet's response to it. Consider the tone established by this poem as an introduction to three books of love poetry.

Support your assertions with references drawn from **throughout** the poem. All Latin words must be copied or their line numbers provided, AND they must be translated or paraphrased closely enough so that it is clear you understand the Latin. It is your responsibility to convince your reader that you are basing your conclusions on the Latin text and not merely on a general recollection of the passage. Direct your answer to the question; do not merely summarize the passage. Please write your essay on a separate piece of paper.

Scansion

Scan the following lines.

Arma gravi numero violentaque bella parabam

    edere, materia conveniente modis.

par erat inferior versus; risisse Cupido

    dicitur atque unum surripuisse pedem.

Vocabulary

The vocabulary exercises require you to provide the dictionary entry for a given Latin word. List nouns by nominative and genitive singular and gender; list adjectives by all nominative singular forms; list verbs by principal parts. In this exercise, also provide the principal meaning for each word. Use the blanks provided for your list. Provide line references in parentheses beside your Latin choices.

1. List ten Latin words in the poem that refer to weapons or war.

    a. _____

    b. _____

    c. _____

    d. _____

    e. _____

    f. _____

    g. _____

    h. _____

    i. _____

    j. _____

2. List the names of nine gods or goddesses in the poem.

   a. _____

   b. _____

   c. _____

   d. _____

   e. _____

   f. _____

   g. _____

   h. _____

   i. _____

3. List five words for parts of the body.

   a. _____

   b. _____

   c. _____

   d. _____

   e. _____

4. List nine words that refer to poetry or poetic meter.

   a. _____

   b. _____

   c. _____

   d. _____

   e. _____

   f. _____

   g. _____

   h. _____

   i. _____

5. List two proper nouns or adjectives that refer to geographic locations.

   a. _____

   b. _____

AMORES 1.3

Iusta precor: quae me nuper praedata puella est,
    aut amet aut faciat, cur ego semper amem.
a, nimium volui: tantum patiatur amari,
    audierit nostras tot Cytherea preces.
5   accipe, per longos tibi qui deserviat annos;
    accipe, qui pura norit amare fide.
si me non veterum commendant magna parentum
    nomina, si nostri sanguinis auctor eques,
nec meus innumeris renovatur campus aratris,
10   temperat et sumptus parcus uterque parens,
at Phoebus comitesque novem vitisque repertor
    hac faciunt et me qui tibi donat Amor
et nulli cessura fides, sine crimine mores,
    nudaque simplicitas purpureusque pudor.
15   non mihi mille placent, non sum desultor amoris:
    tu mihi, si qua fides, cura perennis eris;
tecum, quos dederint annos mihi fila sororum,
    vivere contingat teque dolente mori;
te mihi materiem felicem in carmina praebe:
20   provenient causa carmina digna sua.
carmine nomen habent exterrita cornibus Io
    et quam fluminea lusit adulter ave
quaeque super pontum simulato vecta iuvenco
    virginea tenuit cornua vara manu.
25   nos quoque per totum pariter cantabimur orbem
    iunctaque semper erunt nomina nostra tuis.

Short Answer Questions

Line 1   List all the verbs governed by the subject *puella*. _____

Line 2   Translate *amet*. _____

            Translate *faciat*. _____

Line 3   Translate *patiatur*. _____

            What type of infinitive is *amari* and how is it best translated? _____

Line 6   What is the case and use of *fide*? _____

Line 12   What is the antecedent of *qui*? _____

Line 13   What is the case and use of *nulli*? _____

             From which verb is *cessura* formed? _____

             What type of participle is it? _____

             How is it best translated? _____

Line 16   What is the case and use of *perennis*? _____

Line 17   What is the subject of *dederint*? _____

Line 18   What is the case and use of *teque dolente*? _____

             Translate this phrase. _____

Line 21   What is unusual about Ovid's use of the ablative of *carmine*? _____

             _____

Line 24   Which noun does the adjective *virginea* modify? _____

             Which noun does *vara* modify? _____

Multiple Choice Questions *Suggested time: 10 minutes*

1. The antecedent of *quae* (line 1) is
   a. *iusta*
   b. *praedata*
   c. *puella*
   d. *me*

2. In line 8, what word is missing to make the line syntactically complete?
   a. *sum*
   b. *sunt*
   c. *est*
   d. *sumus*

3. In line 10, we learn that the author's parents are
   a. wealthy
   b. frugal
   c. old
   d. farmers

4. In lines 7–10, Ovid tries to
   a. impress his *puella*
   b. dissuade his *puella*
   c. be modest
   d. attack his *puella*

5. In line 12, what does *Amor* give to the young girl?
   a. the Muses
   b. Bacchus
   c. Ovid
   d. Apollo

6. In line 14, we find an example of
   a. allegory
   b. alliteration
   c. chiasmus
   d. anaphora

7. In line 20, the poet promises his girlfriend that
   a. he will write poems worthy of her
   b. he will pursue her forever in poetry
   c. they will sing the same worthy song
   d. their cause will be worthy of this song

8. The metrical pattern of the first four feet of line 23 is
   a. dactyl-dactyl-dactyl-spondee
   b. dactyl-spondee-dactyl-dactyl
   c. dactyl-spondee-spondee-spondee
   d. dactyl-spondee-dactyl-spondee

Translation *Suggested time: 15 minutes*

Translate the passage below as literally as possible.

> si me non veterum commendant magna parentum
>   nomina, si nostri sanguinis auctor eques,
> nec meus innumeris renovatur campus aratris,
>   temperat et sumptus parcus uterque parens,
> 5 at Phoebus comitesque novem vitisque repertor
>   hac faciunt et me qui tibi donat Amor
> et nulli cessura fides, sine crimine mores,
>   nudaque simplicitas purpureusque pudor.

Short Analyis Questions

1. Why is *Cytherea* (line 4) an appropriate reference to use in this poem?

2. Briefly discuss the effect of the concession of *si qua fides* in line 16.

3. To whom does Ovid refer in line 22 (*et quam . . . ave*)?

4. To whom does Ovid refer in lines 23–24 (*quaeque . . . manu*)?

5. Briefly discuss the relationship between the significant figure of speech and the literal meaning of line 24.

Essay *Suggested time: 20 minutes*

In this poem, Ovid tries to persuade his new girlfriend to love him. In his defense he lists many examples of lovers from the world of mythology. Write an essay in which you discuss the effectiveness of these famous lovers on the poet's argument.

Support your assertions with references drawn from **throughout** the poem. All Latin words must be copied or their line numbers provided, AND they must be translated or paraphrased closely enough so that it is clear you understand the Latin. It is your responsibility to convince your reader that you are basing your conclusions on the Latin text and not merely on a general recollection of the passage. Direct your answer to the question; do not merely summarize the passage. Please write your essay on a separate piece of paper.

Scansion

Scan the following lines.

tecum, quos dederint annos mihi fila sororum,

vivere contingat teque dolente mori;

te mihi materiem felicem in carmina praebe:

provenient causa carmina digna sua.

Vocabulary

Below is a list of high frequency words you have already encountered in *Amores* 1.1 and 1.3. For all the words you know, write out full dictionary entries, including English meanings, and put a √ mark in the left-hand column to show you have already committed these words to memory. For any words you do not yet know, write out the dictionary entries using the end glossary and learn them as soon as possible.

√

1. ____ *accipiō* _____
2. ____ *amō* _____
3. ____ *amor* _____
4. ____ *aut* _____
5. ____ *carmen* _____
6. ____ *dō* _____
7. ____ *ego* _____
8. ____ *et* _____
9. ____ *faciō* _____
10. ____ *habeō* _____
11. ____ *hic* (adjective/pronoun) _____
12. ____ *longus* _____

AMORES 1.3 • 13

13. ____ *magnus* ____
14. ____ *meus* ____
15. ____ *nec* ____
16. ____ *nimium* ____
17. ____ *per* ____
18. ____ *Phoebus* ____
19. ____ *puella* ____
20. ____ *quī* ____
21. ____ *sī* ____
22. ____ *sum* ____
23. ____ *suus* ____
24. ____ *tū* ____
25. ____ *vīvō* ____

AMORES 1.9

Militat omnis amans, et habet sua castra Cupido;
    Attice, crede mihi, militat omnis amans.
quae bello est habilis, Veneri quoque convenit aetas:
    turpe senex miles, turpe senilis amor.
5 quos petiere duces animos in milite forti,
    hos petit in socio bella puella viro:
pervigilant ambo, terra requiescit uterque;
    ille fores dominae servat, at ille ducis.
militis officium longa est via: mitte puellam,
10   strenuus exempto fine sequetur amans;
ibit in adversos montes duplicataque nimbo
    flumina, congestas exteret ille nives,
nec freta pressurus tumidos causabitur Euros
    aptave verrendis sidera quaeret aquis.
15 quis nisi vel miles vel amans et frigora noctis
    et denso mixtas perferet imbre nives?
mittitur infestos alter speculator in hostes,
    in rivale oculos alter, ut hoste, tenet.
ille graves urbes, hic durae limen amicae
20   obsidet; hic portas frangit, at ille fores.
saepe soporatos invadere profuit hostes
    caedere et armata vulgus inerme manu.
sic fera Threicii ceciderunt agmina Rhesi,
    et dominum capti deseruistis equi.
25 nempe maritorum somnis utuntur amantes
    et sua sopitis hostibus arma movent.
custodum transire manus vigilumque catervas
    militis et miseri semper amantis opus.
Mars dubius, nec certa Venus: victique resurgunt,
30   quosque neges umquam posse iacere, cadunt.
ergo desidiam quicumque vocabat amorem,
    desinat: ingenii est experientis Amor.
ardet in abducta Briseide magnus Achilles
    (dum licet, Argeas frangite, Troes, opes);
35 Hector ab Andromaches complexibus ibat ad arma,
    et galeam capiti quae daret, uxor erat;
summa ducum, Atrides visa Priameide fertur
    Maenadis effusis obstipuisse comis.
Mars quoque deprensus fabrilia vincula sensit:
40   notior in caelo fabula nulla fuit.
ipse ego segnis eram discinctaque in otia natus;
    mollierant animos lectus et umbra meos;

> impulit ignavum formosae cura puellae,
> iussit et in castris aera merere suis.
> 45 inde vides agilem nocturnaque bella gerentem:
> qui nolet fieri desidiosus, amet.

Short Answer Questions

Line 3   What are the gender, case, and number of *quae*? _____

Which other word in this line is its antecedent? _____

Line 5   Which word is the subject of *petiere*? _____

Line 8   What is the case and number of *ducis*? _____

On which other noun in the line does it depend? _____

Line 10   Translate *exempto fine*. _____

Line 11   What is the subject of *ibit*? _____

Line 13   What is the case and use of *Euros*? _____

What type of participle is *pressurus*? _____

Why is it nominative masculine singular? _____

How might it best be translated? _____

Line 18   What is the case and use of *hoste*? _____

Line 30   What is the subject of *cadunt*? _____

Line 45   What type of participle is *gerentem*? _____

Why is it accusative singular? _____

How might it best be translated? _____

Multiple Choice Questions *Suggested time: 13 minutes*

1. In line 3, Ovid is making reference to
   a. young men
   b. young women
   c. mature men
   d. mature women

2. What is the figure of speech in line 3?
   a. polysyndeton
   b. antithesis
   c. prolepsis
   d. zeugma

3. What is the antecedent of *ille* (line 12)?
   a. *nives* (line 12)
   b. *amans* (line 10)
   c. *nimbo* (line 11)
   d. *Euros* (line 13)

4. In lines 13–14, Ovid employs examples drawn primarily from
   a. sailing
   b. marching
   c. mountain climbing
   d. drinking

5. The metrical pattern of the first four feet of line 15 is
   a. dactyl-spondee-dactyl-spondee
   b. spondee-dactyl-spondee-dactyl
   c. dactyl-dactyl-dactyl-spondee
   d. dactyl-spondee-spondee-spondee

6. In line 22, to whom does *vulgus* refer?
   a. girl
   b. Cupid
   c. lover
   d. enemy

7. What is the best translation for *visa Priameide* (line 37)?
   a. when Cassandra had been seen
   b. when Cassandra saw
   c. having been seen by Cassandra
   d. with Cassandra having seen him

8. What is the case and number of *fabrilia vincula* (line 39)?
   a. ablative singular
   b. nominative plural
   c. accusative plural
   d. nominative singular

9. In line 44, *suis* refers to
   a. Cupid
   b. Ovid
   c. the lover
   d. *cura* (line 43)

10. What type of subjunctive clause is *nolet* (line 46)?
    a. indirect question
    b. subjunctive by attraction
    c. relative clause of characteristic
    d. indirect command

11. The majority of examples Ovid offers to support his thesis come from
    a. the Trojan War
    b. mythology
    c. Roman love poetry
    d. the history of Rome

Translation *Suggested time: 15 minutes*

Translate the passage below as literally as possible.

> Militat omnis amans, et habet sua castra Cupido;
>   Attice, crede mihi, militat omnis amans.
> quae bello est habilis, Veneri quoque convenit aetas:
>   turpe senex miles, turpe senilis amor.
> 5 quos petiere duces animos in milite forti,
>   hos petit in socio bella puella viro:
> pervigilant ambo, terra requiescit uterque;
>   ille fores dominae servat, at ille ducis.

Short Analysis Questions

1. In lines 9–16, Ovid makes many references to storms and bad weather. Write out and translate two words or phrases that represent adverse conditions. Provide line references in parentheses for your Latin choices.

    a. _____

    b. _____

2. In line 29, Ovid makes reference to *Mars* and *Venus*. Briefly explain why these two gods are significant in this context.

3. Name four heroes of the Trojan War whom Ovid mentions in this poem and briefly explain their relevance to Ovid's argument.

   a. _____

   b. _____

   c. _____

   d. _____

4. a. In line 45, *nocturna bella* represents what figure of speech? _____

   b. To what is Ovid referring with these words? _____

Essay *Suggested time: 20 minutes*

In traditional love poetry, Love/Venus is most frequently contrasted with War/Mars, not compared, as Ovid does in *Amores* 1.9. In a short essay, show how Ovid successfully employs these two deities as similar, not differing, in their purposes, and thus reinforces his theme that every lover is a soldier.

Support your assertions with references drawn from **throughout** the poem. All Latin words must be copied or their line numbers provided, AND they must be translated or paraphrased closely enough so that it is clear you understand the Latin. It is your responsibility to convince your reader that you are basing your conclusions on the Latin text and not merely on a general recollection of the passage. Direct your answer to the question; do not merely summarize the passage. Please write your essay on a separate piece of paper.

Scansion

Scan the following lines.

Mars dubius, nec certa Venus: victique resurgunt,

    quosque neges umquam posse iacere, cadunt.

ergo desidiam quicumque vocabat amorem,

    desinat: ingenii est experientis Amor.

Vocabulary

Below you will find a list of high frequency words you have encountered in your recent readings. For all the words you know, write out full dictionary entries, including English meanings, and put a √ mark in the left-hand column to show you have already committed these words to memory. For any words you do not yet know, write out the dictionary entries using the end glossary and learn them as soon as possible.

      √

1. _____ *ā, ab* _____
2. _____ *ad* _____
3. _____ *aptus* _____
4. _____ *arma* _____
5. _____ *at* _____
6. _____ *bellum* _____
7. _____ *certus* _____
8. _____ *coma* _____
9. _____ *crinis* _____
10. _____ *Cupīdō* _____
11. _____ *dēserviō* _____
12. _____ *gravis* _____

13. ____ *ille* _____

14. ____ *in* _____

15. ____ *manus* _____

16. ____ *Mars* _____

17. ____ *miser* _____

18. ____ *moveō* _____

19. ____ *nullus* _____

20. ____ *opus* _____

21. ____ *quis* _____

22. ____ *quoque* _____

23. ____ *semper* _____

24. ____ *teneō* _____

25. ____ *uterque* _____

26. ____ *Venus* _____

AMORES 1.11

Colligere incertos et in ordine ponere crines
    docta neque ancillas inter habenda Nape
inque ministeriis furtivae cognita noctis
    utilis et dandis ingeniosa notis,
5 saepe venire ad me dubitantem hortata Corinnam,
    saepe laboranti fida reperta mihi,
accipe et ad dominam peraratas mane tabellas
    perfer et obstantes sedula pelle moras.
nec silicum venae nec durum in pectore ferrum
10   nec tibi simplicitas ordine maior adest;
credibile est et te sensisse Cupidinis arcus:
    in me militiae signa tuere tuae.
si quaeret quid agam, spe noctis vivere dices;
    cetera fert blanda cera notata manu.
15 dum loquor, hora fugit: vacuae bene redde tabellas,
    verum continuo fac tamen illa legat.
aspicias oculos mando frontemque legentis:
    et tacito vultu scire futura licet.
nec mora, perlectis rescribat multa iubeto:
20   odi, cum late splendida cera vacat.
comprimat ordinibus versus, oculosque moretur
    margine in extremo littera †rasa† meos.
quid digitos opus est graphio lassare tenendo?
    hoc habeat scriptum tota tabella "veni."
25 non ego victrices lauro redimire tabellas
    nec Veneris media ponere in aede morer.
subscribam VENERI FIDAS SIBI NASO MINISTRAS
    DEDICAT. AT NUPER VILE FUISTIS ACER.

Short Answer Questions

Line 4   What verb form is *dandis*? _____

             What noun does it modify? _____

Line 5   What verb form is *dubitantem*? _____

             What noun does it modify? _____

Line 6   What is the case and use of *laboranti*? _____

Lines 1–6	What are all the adjectives in these lines that modify Nape? Provide line references in parentheses for your Latin choices.

_____

_____

_____

_____

_____

_____

Lines 7–8	What are the three imperatives in these lines? _____
	_____
Line 10	What is the case and use of *tibi*? _____
	What is the case and use of *ordine*? _____
Line 11	What is the case and use of *te*? _____
Line 12	What is the form of *tuere*? _____
Line 13	What is the form of *agam*? _____
	How is *agam* used? _____
	What is the subject of *vivere*? _____
Line 14	What is the subject of *fert*? _____
Line 16	What is the form of *legat*? _____
	How is *legat* used? _____
Line 17	What is the form of *aspicias*? _____
	How is *aspicias* used? _____
Line 21	What is the subject of *moretur*? _____
Line 27	What is the case and use of *Veneri*? _____

Multiple Choice Questions *Suggested time: 15 minutes*

1. The figure of speech employed in *neque ancillas inter habenda* (line 2) is
   a. polysyndeton
   b. ellipsis
   c. hyperbaton
   d. hyperbole

2. Another figure of speech in line 2, *ancillas inter*, is
   a. metaphor
   b. litotes
   c. asyndeton
   d. prolepsis

3. In line 3, *noctis* is called *furtivae* because
   a. Nape is deceptive
   b. Ovid's relationship with Corinna is secretive/improper
   c. Ovid doesn't know when he will see Corinna
   d. night is dark and secretive

4. Ovid tells us in line 9 that
   a. Nape is cruel
   b. Nape is hard-hearted
   c. Nape is soft-hearted
   d. Nape is not made of stone

5. In line 10, Ovid additionally describes Nape as one
   a. who is too ambitious
   b. who is not overly sophisticated for her station
   c. who dresses with simplicity
   d. who comes from the lower class

6. The metrical pattern for the first four feet of line 11 is
   a. spondee-dactyl-spondee-dactyl
   b. dactyl-spondee-dactyl-spondee
   c. dactyl-spondee-spondee-dactyl
   d. spondee-spondee-dactyl-dactyl

7. The figure of speech which Ovid uses in line 12 is
   a. metaphor
   b. personification
   c. pleonasm
   d. metonymy

8. In line 15, *vacuae* modifies
   a. *tabellas*
   b. *hora*
   c. the speaker as indirect object
   d. *dominae* (understood)

9. In lines 17–18, the poet asks
   a. Nape to watch Corinna while she reads the letter
   b. Corinna to be calm
   c. to know the future
   d. to read Corinna's face

10. In lines 19–24, the poet will settle for a reply
    a. that comes right back
    b. that doesn't tire Corinna
    c. that is a single word
    d. that will completely fill the tablet

11. The case of *vile* (line 28) is
    a. ablative singular
    b. nominative plural
    c. accusative plural
    d. nominative singular

12. The poet employs in line 28 the figure of speech known as
    a. assonance
    b. hyperbole
    c. metaphor
    d. personification

Translation *Suggested time: 15 minutes*

Translate the passage below as literally as possible.

>   si quaeret quid agam, spe noctis vivere dices;
>   cetera fert blanda cera notata manu.
>   dum loquor, hora fugit: vacuae bene redde tabellas,
>   verum continuo fac tamen illa legat.
> 5   aspicias oculos mando frontemque legentis:
>   et tacito vultu scire futura licet.
>   nec mora, perlectis rescribat multa iubeto:
>   odi, cum late splendida cera vacat.

Short Analysis Questions

1. In line 10, the poet refers to Nape's *simplicitas*. What characteristic of the maid is he describing here?

   _____

2. a. Write a literal translation of line 11 *credibile est et te sensisse Cupidinis arcus*.

   _____

   b. Why is this line a dubious compliment? _____

   _____

3. To whom does the word *legentis* (line 17) refer? _____

4. What is the Latin word that must be understood in order to complete an ablative absolute with *perlectis* (line 19)?

   _____

5. In lines 25–28, the poet promises to reward the tablets if he gets a favorable reply from Corinna. Name two actions the poet will take and cite the Latin that expresses each.

   _____

   _____

   _____

   _____

   _____

Essay *Suggested time: 20 minutes*

In lines 19–24, Ovid describes the answer that he wishes to receive from Corinna. Write a short essay in which you discuss the contrast between the original reply that Ovid wants and the final reply that he requests. Consider the poet's reason for changing his request in your answer.

Support your assertions with appropriate references drawn from the poem. All Latin words must be copied or their line numbers provided, AND they must be translated or paraphrased closely enough so that it is clear you understand the Latin. It is your responsibility to convince your reader that you are basing your conclusions on the Latin text and not merely on a general recollection of the passage. Direct your answer to the question; do not merely summarize the passage. Please write your essay on a separate piece of paper.

Scansion

Scan the following lines.

credibile est et te sensisse Cupidinis arcus:

    in me militiae signa tuere tuae.

si quaeret quid agam, spe noctis vivere dices;

    cetera fert blanda cera notata manu.

28 • OVID

Vocabulary

1. What two Latin words combine to form *colligo* (line 1)? Give each Latin word and its meaning.

    a. _____

    b. _____

2. Give the principal parts for the verb from which *dandis* (line 4) is formed. Give a meaning for each part.

    a. _____

    b. _____

    c. _____

    d. _____

3. Give the principal parts for the verb from which *hortata* (line 5) is formed. Give a meaning for each part.

    a. _____

    b. _____

    c. _____

4. What two Latin words form *accipe* (line 7)? Give each Latin word and its meaning.

    a. _____

    b. _____

5. Give the principal parts and meanings for *agam* (line 13).

    a. _____

    b. _____

    c. _____

    d. _____

6. Give the principal parts and meanings for *loquor* (line 15).

    a. _____

    b. _____

    c. _____

7. *fac* (line 16) is an irregular imperative. List the three other monosyllabic imperatives in Latin and give their meanings.

   a. _____

   b. _____

   c. _____

8. a. What kind of a verb is *licet* (line 18)? _____

   b. Translate *licet*. _____

9. Give the principal parts and meanings for the verb from which *perlectis* (line 19) is formed.

   a. _____

   b. _____

   c. _____

   d. _____

10. Give the two Latin words and their meanings that combine to create this verb.

    a. _____

    b. _____

11. Give the principal parts and meanings for *morer* (line 26).

    a. _____

    b. _____

    c. _____

AMORES 1.12

Flete meos casus: tristes rediere tabellae;
    infelix hodie littera posse negat.
omina sunt aliquid: modo cum discedere vellet,
    ad limen digitos restitit icta Nape.
5 missa foras iterum limen transire memento
    cautius atque alte sobria ferre pedem.
ite hinc, difficiles, funebria ligna, tabellae,
    tuque, negaturis cera referta notis,
quam, puto, de longae collectam flore cicutae
10   melle sub infami Corsica misit apis.
at tamquam minio penitus medicata rubebas:
    ille color vere sanguinulentus erat.
proiectae triviis iaceatis, inutile lignum,
    vosque rotae frangat praetereuntis onus.
15 illum etiam, qui vos ex arbore vertit in usum,
    convincam puras non habuisse manus.
praebuit illa arbor misero suspendia collo,
    carnifici diras praebuit illa cruces;
illa dedit turpes raucis bubonibus umbras,
20   vulturis in ramis et strigis ova tulit.
his ego commisi nostros insanus amores
    molliaque ad dominam verba ferenda dedi?
aptius hae capiant vadimonia garrula cerae,
    quas aliquis duro cognitor ore legat;
25 inter ephemeridas melius tabulasque iacerent,
    in quibus absumptas fleret avarus opes.
ergo ego vos rebus duplices pro nomine sensi:
    auspicii numerus non erat ipse boni.
quid precer iratus, nisi vos cariosa senectus
30   rodat, et immundo cera sit alba situ?

Short Answer Questions

Line 1	What is the form of *rediere*? _____
	What is its subject? _____
Line 2	The subject for the infinitive *posse* is missing. What is the subject? _____
	What complementary infinitive for *posse* is missing? _____
Line 3	What is the form of *vellet*? _____
	How is this form used? _____
Line 4	What is the case and use of *digitos*? _____
Line 8	What is the case and use of the two words *negaturis . . . notis*? _____
	What is the form of *negaturis*? _____
	Translate the two words *negaturis . . . notis*. _____
Line 11	What is the form of *medicata*? _____
	What does it modify? _____
Line 13	What is the form of *iaceatis*? _____
	How is this form used? _____
	Translate *iaceatis*. _____
Line 14	What is the form of *praetereuntis*? _____
	Of which irregular verb is this a compound? _____
Line 15	What is the case and use of *illum*? _____
Line 18	What is the case and use of *carnifici*? _____
Line 22	What is the form of *ferenda*? _____
	Translate *ferenda*. _____
Line 24	What is the antecedent for *quas*? _____
	What is the form of *legat*? _____
	How is this form used? _____
Line 28	What is the case and use of the two words *auspicii . . . boni*? _____
Line 29	What is the form of *precer*? _____
	How is this form used? _____

Multiple Choice Questions *Suggested time: 13 minutes*

1. Whom does the poet address in *flete* (line 1)?
   a. Corinna
   b. Nape
   c. his audience/readers
   d. Corinna and Nape together

2. Why does the poet call the tablets *funebria ligna* (line 7)?
   a. the wood is poisonous
   b. the wood is unlucky
   c. the poet wants to die
   d. Corinna has died

3. What is the figure of speech used in lines 7 and 11?
   a. hyperbole
   b. metonymy
   c. plenonasm
   d. personification

4. Why does the poet call the wood *inutile* (line 13)?
   a. the tablets have failed to carry back a favorable message
   b. the wood of the tablets cannot be used again
   c. the wood of the tablets has been broken
   d. the wood of the tablets has been thrown away

5. In line 19, the word order is a poetic figure of speech called
   a. golden line
   b. interlocked
   c. chiasmus
   d. ellipsis

6. The poet is *insanus* in line 21 because
   a. he committed his words to the tablets
   b. he entrusted his love to the tablets
   c. Corinna does not love him
   d. his message was too gentle

7. The metrical pattern for the first four feet of line 23 is
   a. dactyl-dactyl-dactyl-dactyl
   b. dactyl-spondee-dactyl-dactyl
   c. spondee-dactyl-spondee-dactyl
   d. dactyl-dactyl-dactyl-spondee

8. From lines 27–28, we learn that the poet calls the tablets *duplices* because
   a. they are deceitful
   b. they are cruel
   c. they are made of wax
   d. they have two halves

9. The poet is *iratus* in line 29 because
   a. the tablets were unlucky
   b. he cannot visit Corinna tonight
   c. the tablets are eroding
   d. the wax has turned white

10. In line 29, *nisi* is best translated as
    a. unless
    b. if not that
    c. so that
    d. except that

11. The adjective *alba* (line 30) contrasts to the wax's original color which was
    a. blue
    b. red
    c. black
    d. yellow

Translation *Suggested time: 10 minutes*

Translate the passage below as literally as possible.

> **his ego commisi nostros insanus amores**
> **molliaque ad dominam verba ferenda dedi?**
> **aptius hae capiant vadimonia garrula cerae,**
> **quas aliquis duro cognitor ore legat;**
> 5 **inter ephemeridas melius tabulasque iacerent,**
> **in quibus absumptas fleret avarus opes.**

Short Analysis Questions

1. a. Translate lines 3–6.

   > omina sunt aliquid: modo cum discedere vellet,
   >   ad limen digitos restitit icta Nape.
   > 5   missa foras iterum limen transire memento
   >   cautius atque alte sobria ferre pedem.

   b. Explain exactly to what real omen the poet refers in these lines.

2. In lines 7–10, the poet curses the tablets and the wax.

   a. Give two Latin examples of how the wax is cursed. Translate your examples.

   b. Explain *melle sub infami* (line 10). How can the wax be sent under the honey?

3. In line 13, the poet suggests that the tablets be cast out at the crossroads, the meeting of three ways. To what might this be a reference?

4. In lines 15–20, the poet gives four reasons why the wood is unlucky. State two of the reasons, giving the Latin and translating it:

   a. _____

   b. _____

5. What are the best uses of the tablets according to lines 23–26? Use Latin words in your response.

   a. _____

   _____

   b. _____

   _____

6. How do the uses described in lines 23–26 contrast to those for which the poet employed the tablets?

   _____

   _____

   _____

   _____

   _____

Essay *Suggested time: 20 minutes*

Amores 1.11 and 1.12 are a pair, written to be read as a unit. Write an essay in which you compare the personification of the tablets in both poems. Pay particular attention to the poet's promise in 1.11.27–28 and his prayer in 1.12.29–30. How do these contrasting personifications affect the two poems?

Support your assertions with references drawn from **throughout** both poems. All Latin words must be copied or their line numbers provided, AND they must be translated or paraphrased closely enough so that it is clear you understand the Latin. It is your responsibility to convince your reader that you are basing your conclusions on the Latin text and not merely on a general recollection of the passage. Direct your answer to the question; do not merely summarize the passage. Please write your essay on a separate piece of paper.

Scansion

Scan the following lines.

ergo ego vos rebus duplices pro nomine sensi:

auspicii numerus non erat ipse boni.

quid precer iratus, nisi vos cariosa senectus

rodat, et immundo cera sit alba situ?

Vocabulary

List the nouns, adjectives, and verbs with negative connotations in this poem. Provide the dictionary entry for the words you list. List the participles as adjectives. Provide line references in parentheses beside your Latin choices.

Nouns

1. _____
2. _____
3. _____
4. _____
5. _____
6. _____
7. _____
8. _____
9. _____
10. _____
11. _____
12. _____
13. _____
14. _____

Adjectives

1. _____
2. _____
3. _____
4. _____
5. _____
6. _____
7. _____
8. _____
9. _____
10. _____
11. _____
12. _____
13. _____
14. _____
15. _____
16. _____
17. _____
18. _____
19. _____
20. _____
21. _____

Verbs

1. _____
2. _____
3. _____
4. _____
5. _____

AMORES 3.15

Quaere novum vatem, tenerorum mater Amorum:
    raditur haec elegis ultima meta meis;
quos ego composui, Paeligni ruris alumnus,
    (nec me deliciae dedecuere meae)
5 si quid id est, usque a proavis vetus ordinis heres,
    non modo militiae turbine factus eques.
Mantua Vergilio gaudet, Verona Catullo;
    Paelignae dicar gloria gentis ego,
quam sua libertas ad honesta coegerat arma,
10   cum timuit socias anxia Roma manus.
atque aliquis spectans hospes Sulmonis aquosi
    moenia, quae campi iugera pauca tenent,
"quae tantum" dicet "potuistis ferre poetam,
    quantulacumque estis, vos ego magna voco."
15 culte puer puerique parens Amathusia culti,
    aurea de campo vellite signa meo:
corniger increpuit thyrso graviore Lyaeus;
    pulsanda est magnis area maior equis.
imbelles elegi, genialis Musa, valete,
20   post mea mansurum fata superstes opus.

Short Answer Questions

Line 1	What is the form of *quaere*?
Line 2	What is the case and use of the two words *elegis . . . meis*?
Line 3	What is the case and use of *quos*?
Line 4	What is the form of *dedecuere*?
	What is the case and use of the two words *deliciae . . . meae*?
Line 7	What is the case and use of *Vergilio* and *Catullo*?
Line 9	What is the antecedent for *quam*?
	What is the case and use of *quam*?
Line 12	What is the case and use of *campi*?
Line 13	What is the antecedent for *quae*?
	What is the case and use of *quae*?

Line 16   What is the form of *vellite*? _____

Line 17   What is the case and use of *thyrso graviore*? _____

Line 18   What is the form of *pulsanda*? _____

Line 20   What is the form of *mansurum*? _____

Multiple Choice Questions *Suggested time: 12 minutes*

1. Whom does the poet address in *quaere* (line 1)?
   - a. his mother
   - b. Venus
   - c. Corinna
   - d. Cupid

2. Line 2 (*raditur . . . meis*) is best translated as
   - a. the final goal post is grazed by my elegies
   - b. I have grazed the final goal post with my elegies
   - c. my elegies have grazed the final goal post
   - d. these are my final elegies at the goal post

3. The case of *deliciae* in line 4 is
   - a. nominative
   - b. genitive
   - c. dative
   - d. vocative

4. The metrical pattern of the first four feet of line 13 is
   - a. dactyl-spondee-dactyl-spondee
   - b. spondee-dactyl-dactyl-spondee
   - c. spondee-spondee-dactyl-spondee
   - d. spondee-dactyl-spondee-dactyl

5. In line 15, the words *culte* and *culti* represent what figure of speech?
   - a. hyperbaton
   - b. polyptoton
   - c. hendiadys
   - d. hysteron proteron

6. In line 16, *vellite* is directed towards
   - a. Apollo
   - b. Cupid
   - c. Venus and Apollo
   - d. Cupid and Venus

7. In line 16, *campo meo* is an ablative of
   - a. manner
   - b. separation
   - c. instrument
   - d. comparison

8. To what god does *corniger Lyaeus* (line 17) refer?
   - a. Mars
   - b. Venus
   - c. Cupid
   - d. Bacchus

9. When the poet refers to *magnis area maior equis* (line 18) he means
   a. that he is going to drive a team of horses
   b. that his poetry will be concerned with greater love
   c. that he will travel to great lands
   d. that he will undertake a new and grander kind of poetry

10. Line 20 (*post . . . opus*) is best translated:
    a. [farewell] my work which will remain after my fates
    b. [farewell] my surviving work which will remain after my death
    c. [farewell] after my death you will remain my work
    d. [farewell] you who will not remain fated after my work

Translation *Suggested time: 15 minutes*

Translate the passage below as literally as possible.

      Mantua Vergilio gaudet, Verona Catullo;
          Paelignae dicar gloria gentis ego,
      quam sua libertas ad honesta coegerat arma,
          cum timuit socias anxia Roma manus.
5   atque aliquis spectans hospes Sulmonis aquosi
          moenia, quae campi iugera pauca tenent,
      "quae tantum" dicet "potuistis ferre poetam,
          quantulacumque estis, vos ego magna voco."

Short Analysis Questions

1. What are the two meanings for *deliciae* in line 4?

    a. _____

    b. _____

2. In line 6, the poet refers to the *militiae turbine*. What does this phrase mean literally and why does Ovid view it as inappropriate for himself?

    _____

    _____

3. To what historical event does line 10 *cum timuit socias anxia Roma manus* refer?

    _____

4. Translate *aurea de campo vellite signa meo* (line 16).

    _____

5. Who is the *genialis Musa* referred to in line 19?

    _____

Essay *Suggested time: 20 minutes*

This poem, the last of the *Amores*, contains the poet's farewell to elegiac poetry and articulates his intention to write tragic poetry. The poem contains, as well, the poet's assessment of what he has accomplished. Write a short essay in which you summarize Ovid's self-evaluation of his and his poetry's worth.

Support your assertions with references drawn from **throughout** the poem. All Latin words must be copied or their line numbers provided, AND they must be translated or paraphrased closely enough so that it is clear you understand the Latin. It is your responsibility to convince your reader that you are basing your conclusions on the Latin text and not merely on a general recollection of the passage. Direct your answer to the question; do not merely summarize the passage. Please write your essay on a separate piece of paper.

Scansion

Scan the following lines.

Quaere novum vatem, tenerorum mater Amorum:

    raditur haec elegis ultima meta meis;

quos ego composui, Paeligni ruris alumnus,

    (nec me deliciae dedecuere meae)

Vocabulary

1. List the six nouns in the poem that identify the poet. Provide the dictionary entry and principal meaning for the words you list. Provide line references in parentheses beside each Latin noun.

    a. _____
    b. _____
    c. _____
    d. _____
    e. _____
    f. _____

2. List the six adjectives relating to physical or metaphorical size or weight in the poem. Provide the dictionary entry and principal meaning for the words you list. Provide line references in parentheses beside each Latin adjective.

    a. _____
    b. _____
    c. _____
    d. _____
    e. _____
    f. _____

3. List the four participles in the poem. Give an exact translation for each participle and provide the principal parts of the verb from which each comes. Provide line references in parentheses beside each Latin participle.

   a. _____

   b. _____

   c. _____

   d. _____

4. List the five verbs in the perfect or pluperfect tense in the poem. Translate the form and give the principal parts for its verb. Provide line references in parentheses beside each Latin verb.

   a. _____

   b. _____

   c. _____

   d. _____

   e. _____

5. Provide the dictionary entry and English meaning for each of the following.

   a. *meta* _____

   b. *proavis* _____

   c. *ordinis* _____

   d. *heres* _____

   e. *eques* _____

   f. *hospes* _____

   g. *iugera* _____

   h. *thyrsō* _____

TEXT SELECTIONS FROM THE *METAMORPHOSES* WITH EXERCISES

APOLLO AND DAPHNE
METAMORPHOSES 1.452–487

      Primus amor Phoebi Daphne Peneia, quem non
      fors ignara dedit, sed saeva Cupidinis ira,
      Delius hunc nuper, victa serpente superbus,
455 viderat adducto flectentem cornua nervo
      "quid" que "tibi, lascive puer, cum fortibus armis?"
      dixerat: "ista decent umeros gestamina nostros,
      qui dare certa ferae, dare vulnera possumus hosti,
      qui modo pestifero tot iugera ventre prementem
460 stravimus innumeris tumidum Pythona sagittis.
      tu face nescio quos esto contentus amores
      inritare tua, nec laudes adsere nostras!"
      filius huic Veneris "figat tuus omnia, Phoebe,
      te meus arcus" ait; "quantoque animalia cedunt
465 cuncta deo, tanto minor est tua gloria nostra."
      dixit et eliso percussis aere pennis
      inpiger umbrosa Parnasi constitit arce
      eque sagittifera prompsit duo tela pharetra
      diversorum operum: fugat hoc, facit illud amorem;
470 quod facit, auratum est et cuspide fulget acuta,
      quod fugat, obtusum est et habet sub harundine plumbum.
      hoc deus in nympha Peneide fixit, at illo
      laesit Apollineas traiecta per ossa medullas;
      protinus alter amat, fugit altera nomen amantis
475 silvarum latebris captivarumque ferarum
      exuviis gaudens innuptaeque aemula Phoebes:
      vitta coercebat positos sine lege capillos.
      multi illam petiere, illa aversata petentes
      inpatiens expersque viri nemora avia lustrat
480 nec, quid Hymen, quid Amor, quid sint conubia curat.
      saepe pater dixit: "generum mihi, filia, debes,"
      saepe pater dixit: "debes mihi, nata, nepotes";
      illa velut crimen taedas exosa iugales
      pulchra verecundo suffuderat ora rubore
485 inque patris blandis haerens cervice lacertis
      "da mihi perpetua, genitor carissime," dixit
      "virginitate frui! dedit hoc pater ante Dianae."

APOLLO AND DAPHNE: METAMORPHOSES 1.452–487 • 47

Short Answer Questions

Line 454   What grammatical construction does *victa serpente* form?

_____

Line 458   What is the case and use of *hosti*? _____

Line 462   What word does *tua* modify? _____

Line 464   Of which verb is *te* the accusative direct object? _____

Line 468   What is the case and use of *duo*? _____

                What is the case and use of *pharetra*? _____

Line 474   To whom does *alter* refer? _____

                To whom does *altera* refer? _____

Line 478   What are the person, number, and tense of *petiere*? _____

_____

                To whom does *illa* refer? _____

Line 484   What is the case and use of *ora*? _____

Multiple Choice Questions *Suggested time: 12 minutes*

1. In lines 452–453, we learn that
   a. Cupid is responsible for Apollo's love for Daphne
   b. Daphne's father, Peneus, is responsible for the love between Apollo and Daphne
   c. Apollo fell in love with Daphne by chance
   d. Apollo was the first ever to love Daphne

2. In line 455, *flectentem* refers to
   a. Daphne
   b. Apollo
   c. Delius
   d. Cupid

3. The metrical pattern for the first four feet of line 456 is
   a. dactyl-spondee-dactyl-spondee
   b. dactyl-dactyl-spondee-dactyl
   c. spondee-spondee-dactyl-dactyl
   d. dactyl-spondee-dactyl-dactyl

4. In line 459, *prementem* describes
   a. *qui* (line 459)
   b. *iugera* (line 459)
   c. *tumidum* (line 460)
   d. *Pythona* (line 460)

5. Which of the following figures of speech can be found in lines 461–462 (*tu face . . . inritare tua*)?
   a. hysteron proteron
   b. hyperbaton
   c. hendiadys
   d. hyperbole

6. The best translation for the two words *nec . . . adsere* (line 462) is
   a. not to lay claim to
   b. they did not lay claim to
   c. they have not laid claim to
   d. do not lay claim to

7. The intent of Cupid's speech to Apollo in lines 463–465 (*figat . . . nostra*) is
   a. to boast to Apollo
   b. to glorify Apollo
   c. to advise Apollo
   d. to confuse Apollo

8. The antecedent of *quod* (line 470) is
   a. *operum* (line 469)
   b. *pharetra* (line 468)
   c. *tela* (line 468)
   d. *amorem* (line 469)

9. In line 476, *gaudens* refers to
   a. Daphne
   b. Apollo
   c. hiding places
   d. animal skins

10. In line 478, *aversata* is best translated
    a. rejecting
    b. having been rejected
    c. having rejected
    d. being rejected

Translation *Suggested time: 10 minutes*

Translate the passage below as literally as possible.

> hoc deus in nympha Peneide fixit, at illo
> laesit Apollineas traiecta per ossa medullas;
> protinus alter amat, fugit altera nomen amantis
> silvarum latebris captivarumque ferarum
> 5   exuviis gaudens innuptaeque aemula Phoebes:
> vitta coercebat positos sine lege capillos.

Short Analysis Questions

1. Without translating, briefly state what we learn about Apollo in these words: *victa serpente superbus* (line 454).

2. Identify a synchesis in line 458. Write out the Latin that expresses it and explain why it qualifies as a synchesis.

3. Explain the action that happens in lines 466–469.

Vocabulary

Below you will find a list of high frequency words you have encountered in your recent readings. For all the words you know, write out full dictionary entries, including English meanings, and put a √ mark in the left-hand column to show you have already committed these words to memory. For any words you do not yet know, write out the dictionary entries using the end glossary and learn them as soon as possible.

√

1. _____ alter _____
2. _____ ambō _____
3. _____ atque _____
4. _____ campus _____
5. _____ capillus _____
6. _____ cēdō _____
7. _____ cornū _____
8. _____ crimen _____
9. _____ domina _____
10. _____ durus _____
11. _____ ferus _____
12. _____ fīgō _____
13. _____ gaudeō _____
14. _____ legō _____
15. _____ mittō _____
16. _____ modo _____
17. _____ multus _____
18. _____ negō _____
19. _____ nōmen _____
20. _____ nōn _____
21. _____ nuper _____

22. ____ ōs _____
23. ____ petō _____
24. ____ pharetra _____
25. ____ possum _____
26. ____ premō _____
27. ____ prīmus _____
28. ____ puer _____
29. ____ saepe _____
30. ____ silva _____
31. ____ sine _____
32. ____ tuus _____
33. ____ vincō _____

APOLLO AND DAPHNE
METAMORPHOSES 1.488–524

        ille quidem obsequitur, sed te decor iste quod optas
        esse vetat, votoque tuo tua forma repugnat:
490   Phoebus amat visaeque cupit conubia Daphnes,
        quodque cupit, sperat, suaque illum oracula fallunt,
        utque leves stipulae demptis adolentur aristis,
        ut facibus saepes ardent, quas forte viator
        vel nimis admovit vel iam sub luce reliquit,
495   sic deus in flammas abiit, sic pectore toto
        uritur et sterilem sperando nutrit amorem.
        spectat inornatos collo pendere capillos
        et "quid, si comantur?" ait. videt igne micantes
        sideribus similes oculos, videt oscula, quae non
500   est vidisse satis; laudat digitosque manusque
        bracchiaque et nudos media plus parte lacertos;
        si qua latent, meliora putat. fugit ocior aura
        illa levi neque ad haec revocantis verba resistit:
        "nympha, precor, Penei, mane! non insequor hostis;
505   nympha, mane! sic agna lupum, sic cerva leonem,
        sic aquilam penna fugiunt trepidante columbae,
        hostes quaeque suos: amor est mihi causa sequendi!
        me miserum! ne prona cadas indignave laedi
        crura notent sentes et sim tibi causa doloris!
510   aspera, qua properas, loca sunt: moderatius, oro,
        curre fugamque inhibe, moderatius insequar ipse.
        cui placeas, inquire tamen: non incola montis,
        non ego sum pastor, non hic armenta gregesque
        horridus observo. nescis, temeraria, nescis,
515   quem fugias, ideoque fugis: mihi Delphica tellus
        et Claros et Tenedos Patareaque regia servit;
        Iuppiter est genitor; per me, quod eritque fuitque
        estque, patet; per me concordant carmina nervis.
        certa quidem nostra est, nostra tamen una sagitta
520   certior, in vacuo quae vulnera pectore fecit!
        inventum medicina meum est, opiferque per orbem
        dicor, et herbarum subiecta potentia nobis.
        ei mihi, quod nullis amor est sanabilis herbis
        nec prosunt domino, quae prosunt omnibus, artes!"

Short Answer Questions

Line 493 What is the antecedent of *quas*? _____

Line 498 Translate *comantur*. _____

What is the case and use of *igne*? _____

Line 500 What type of infinitive is *vidisse*? _____

How might it best be translated? _____

Line 502 What is the full form for *qua*? _____

What is the expressed subject of *fugit*? _____

Line 503 What type of participle is *revocantis*? _____

From which verb is it formed? _____

What is its case and use? _____

Line 506 What nouns are subjects of *fugiunt*? Provide line references in parentheses for your Latin choices.

_____

_____

Line 511 What are the person, number, tense, and mood of *curre* and *inhibe*?

_____

Line 522 What are the person, number, tense, voice, and mood of *dicor*?

_____

Translate *dicor*. _____

Multiple Choice Questions *Suggested time: 12 minutes*

1. From lines 488–489, we understand that
   a. Daphne's father will refuse her request
   b. Daphne's beauty will not allow her to remain a virgin
   c. Apollo agrees to stop his pursuit
   d. Apollo continues to pursue Daphne

2. The metrical pattern for the first four metrical feet of line 491 is
   a. dactyl-spondee-dactyl-spondee
   b. dactyl-dactyl-spondee-dactyl
   c. spondee-spondee-dactyl-dactyl
   d. dactyl-spondee-dactyl-dactyl

3. The intent of the simile in lines 492–494 is to compare the burning of torches and fields to
   a. the heat of the sun driven by Phoebus Apollo
   b. the speed of Apollo's pursuit
   c. the depth of Apollo's passion
   d. the countryside through which Apollo and Daphne run

4. In line 493, *ut* is translated
   a. when
   b. in order that
   c. since
   d. just as

5. The repeated use of *–que* in lines 500–501 represents which figure of speech?
   a. polyptoton
   b. prolepsis
   c. polysyndeton
   d. ellipsis

6. In line 507, *sequendi* is a
   a. gerundive
   b. gerund
   c. present participle
   d. present passive infinitive

7. The intent of lines 515–518 is to
   a. impress Daphne
   b. impress the reader with Ovid's knowledge
   c. persuade Apollo to stop running
   d. provide solemnity

8. The figure of speech found in lines 517–518 is
   a. prolepsis
   b. personification
   c. zeugma
   d. polyptoton

9. In line 519, the case of *una* is
   a. accusative
   b. ablative
   c. nominative
   d. dative

10. The best translation of line 523 (*nullis . . . herbis*) is
    a. love is curable by no plants
    b. no love is curable with plants
    c. love is curable by all plants
    d. love has cures with plants

Translation *Suggested time: 15 minutes*

Translate the passage below as literally as possible.

> cui placeas, inquire tamen: non incola montis,
> non ego sum pastor, non hic armenta gregesque
> horridus observo. nescis, temeraria, nescis,
> quem fugias, ideoque fugis: mihi Delphica tellus
> 5 et Claros et Tenedos Patareaque regia servit;
> Iuppiter est genitor; per me, quod eritque fuitque
> estque, patet; per me concordant carmina nervis.

Short Analysis Questions

1. How do the phrases *sed te decor iste quod optas/ esse vetat* and *votoque tuo tua forma repugnat* (lines 488–89) raise the level of pathos in this scene?

2. How does the phrase *suaque illum oracula fallunt* (line 491) raise the level of pathos in this scene?

56 • OVID

3. Write out and identify a synchesis in lines 502–503.

    _____

    _____

4. To what earlier event is Apollo referring with the words *nostra tamen una sagitta certior* (lines 519–520)?

    _____

    _____

Vocabulary

Below you will find a list of high frequency words you have encountered in your recent readings. For all the words you know, write out full dictionary entries, including English meanings, and put a √ mark in the left-hand column to show you have already committed these words to memory. For any words you do not yet know, write out the dictionary entries using the end glossary and learn them as soon as possible.

√

1. _____ *aliquis* _____
2. _____ *ardeō* _____
3. _____ *cadō* _____
4. _____ *causa* _____
5. _____ *collum* _____
6. _____ *dīcō* _____
7. _____ *digitus* _____
8. _____ *herba* _____
9. _____ *hostis* _____
10. _____ *iam* _____
11. _____ *laedō* _____
12. _____ *maneō* _____
13. _____ *mors* _____
14. _____ *nervus* _____
15. _____ *nesciō* _____
16. _____ *noster* _____

17. _____ *nympha* _____
18. _____ *omnis* _____
19. _____ *orbis* _____
20. _____ *precor* _____
21. _____ *prōsum* _____
22. _____ *putō* _____
23. _____ *sagitta* _____
24. _____ *tōtus* _____
25. _____ *vacuus* _____
26. _____ *vel* _____
27. _____ *videō* _____
28. _____ *vulnus* _____

APOLLO AND DAPHNE
METAMORPHOSES 1.525–567

525   Plura locuturum timido Peneia cursu
    fugit cumque ipso verba inperfecta reliquit,
    tum quoque visa decens; nudabant corpora venti,
    obviaque adversas vibrabant flamina vestes,
    et levis inpulsos retro dabat aura capillos,
530   auctaque forma fuga est. sed enim non sustinet ultra
    perdere blanditias iuvenis deus, utque monebat
    ipse Amor, admisso sequitur vestigia passu.
    ut canis in vacuo leporem cum Gallicus arvo
    vidit, et hic praedam pedibus petit, ille salutem;
535   alter inhaesuro similis iam iamque tenere
    sperat et extento stringit vestigia rostro,
    alter in ambiguo est, an sit conprensus, et ipsis
    morsibus eripitur tangentiaque ora relinquit:
    sic deus et virgo est hic spe celer, illa timore.
540   qui tamen insequitur pennis adiutus Amoris,
    ocior est requiemque negat tergoque fugacis
    inminet et crinem sparsum cervicibus adflat.
    viribus absumptis expalluit illa citaeque
    victa labore fugae spectans Peneidas undas
545*   "fer, pater," inquit "opem! si flumina numen habetis,
547   qua nimium placui, mutando perde figuram!"
    vix prece finita torpor gravis occupat artus,
    mollia cinguntur tenui praecordia libro,
550   in frondem crines, in ramos bracchia crescunt,
    pes modo tam velox pigris radicibus haeret,
    ora cacumen habet: remanet nitor unus in illa.
        Hanc quoque Phoebus amat positaque in stipite dextra
    sentit adhuc trepidare novo sub cortice pectus
555   conplexusque suis ramos ut membra lacertis
    oscula dat ligno; refugit tamen oscula lignum.
    cui deus "at, quoniam coniunx mea non potes esse,
    arbor eris certe" dixit "mea! semper habebunt
    te coma, te citharae, te nostrae, laure, pharetrae;
560   tu ducibus Latiis aderis, cum laeta Triumphum

---

* The lack of a line 546 is due to uncertainties and inaccuracies in the ancient texts.

vox canet et visent longas Capitolia pompas;
postibus Augustis eadem fidissima custos
ante fores stabis mediamque tuebere quercum,
utque meum intonsis caput est iuvenale capillis,
565　tu quoque perpetuos semper gere frondis honores!"
finierat Paean: factis modo laurea ramis
adnuit utque caput visa est agitasse cacumen.

Short Answer Questions

Line 525　　　　Of which verb is *plura* the direct object? _____

Lines 533–534　What is the antecedent of *hic*? _____

　　　　　　　What is the antecedent of *ille*? _____

Line 535　　　　What is the form of *inhaesuro*? _____

　　　　　　　What is the case and use of *inhaesuro*? _____

　　　　　　　To whom does *alter* refer? _____

Line 537　　　　To whom does *alter* refer? _____

Line 540　　　　Whom does *adiutus* describe? _____

Line 541　　　　To whom does *fugacis* refer? _____

Line 545　　　　What is the form of *fer*? _____

Line 547　　　　What is the form of *mutando*? _____

　　　　　　　What is the case and use of *mutando*? _____

Line 559　　　　What is the case of *laure*? _____

Lines 560–561　What is the tense of *aderis, canet,* and *visent*? _____

Line 566　　　　What grammatical construction do the two words *factis . . . ramis* form?

_____

Multiple Choice Questions *Suggested time: 12 minutes*

1. In lines 525–526, we learn that
   a. Apollo said many things to Daphne
   b. Daphne fled before Apollo could say many things to her
   c. Apollo was too shy to speak to Daphne
   d. Daphne said many things to Apollo as she fled

2. Line 528 makes use of
   a. synchesis
   b. assonance
   c. golden line
   d. all of the above

3. In line 533, *ut* introduces a(n)
   a. result clause
   b. purpose clause
   c. simile
   d. indirect command

4. *perde* in line 547 is a
   a. second singular imperative verb
   b. first singular present tense subjunctive verb
   c. first singular future tense indicative verb
   d. third singular present tense indicative verb

5. The most literal translation for *vix prece finita* in line 548 is
   a. having hardly finished her prayer
   b. hardly finishing her prayer
   c. her prayer hardly having been finished
   d. her prayer hardly finishing

6. The best translation for line 555 (*complexus . . . lacertis*) is
   a. having embraced with his arms her branches as though limbs
   b. having embraced her arms with his limbs as branches
   c. having been embraced with her arms as limbs
   d. her branches having been embraced as limbs with his arms

7. In line 556, we learn that
   a. Daphne welcomes his kisses
   b. Daphne returns his kisses
   c. Apollo shuns Daphne's kisses
   d. Daphne recoils from his kisses

8. Lines 560–561 refer to the future duties of the laurel/bay at
   a. weddings
   b. civic ceremonies
   c. legal proceedings
   d. military ceremonies

9. The best translation for line 564 (*utque . . . capillis*) is
   a. in order for my youthful head to be unshaven
   b. as my head is youthful with unshaven hair
   c. as my head is unshaven with youthful hair
   d. so that my head remain youthful with unshaven hair

10. The metrical pattern of the first four feet of line 567 is
    a. dactyl-dactyl-dactyl-dactyl
    b. dactyl-dactyl-dactyl-spondee
    c. dactyl-spondee-dactyl-dactyl
    d. dactyl-dactyl-spondee-dactyl

Translation *Suggested time: 15 minutes*

Translate the passage below as literally as possible.

> ut canis in vacuo leporem cum Gallicus arvo
> vidit, et hic praedam pedibus petit, ille salutem;
> alter inhaesuro similis iam iamque tenere
> sperat et extento stringit vestigia rostro,
> 5 alter in ambiguo est, an sit conprensus, et ipsis
> morsibus eripitur tangentiaque ora relinquit:
> sic deus et virgo est hic spe celer, illa timore.

Short Analysis Questions

1. a. Write out and identify a synchesis in line 529.

   b. Briefly explain its possible effect on the meaning of the line.

2. Cite the Latin that incorporates two antonyms in line 551 and briefly examine their effect on the line.

3. Briefly discuss the effect of the tricolon crescendo on line 559.

Essay *Suggested time: 20 minutes*

In this first erotic tale of the *Metamorphoses,* Ovid juxtaposes two motifs: hunting and sexual passion. These manifest themselves at times as hunter and lover and at other times as hunter and hunted. In a short essay explore these seemingly opposing roles. Where do they show up together in the same character and when do they belong only to Apollo or Daphne? Do the characters ever reverse their roles?

Support your assertions with references drawn from **throughout** lines 452–567. All Latin words must be copied or their line numbers provided, AND they must be translated or paraphrased closely enough so that it is clear you understand the Latin. It is your responsibility to convince your reader that you are basing your conclusions on the Latin text and not merely on a general recollection of the passage. Direct your answer to the question; do not merely summarize the passage. Please write your essay on a separate piece of paper.

Scansion

Scan the following lines.

inventum medicina meum est, opiferque per orbem

dicor, et herbarum subiecta potentia nobis.

ei mihi, quod nullis amor est sanabilis herbis

nec prosunt domino, quae prosunt omnibus, artes!"

Vocabulary

Below you will find a list of high frequency words you have encountered in your recent readings. For all the words you know, write out full dictionary entries, including English meanings, and put a √ mark in the left-hand column to show you have already committed these words to memory. For any words you do not yet know, write out the dictionary entries using the end glossary and learn them as soon as possible.

√

1. _____ adsum _____
2. _____ an _____
3. _____ arbor _____
4. _____ arvum _____
5. _____ aura _____
6. _____ blanditia _____
7. _____ caput _____
8. _____ cervix _____
9. _____ deus _____
10. _____ fīdus _____
11. _____ forma _____
12. _____ frons _____
13. _____ fuga _____
14. _____ fugiō _____
15. _____ gerō _____
16. _____ ipse _____
17. _____ lacertus _____
18. _____ levis _____
19. _____ medius _____
20. _____ nūdus _____
21. _____ pectus _____

22. _____ *penna* _____
23. _____ *placeō* _____
24. _____ *sed* _____
25. _____ *sequor* _____
26. _____ *sīc* _____
27. _____ *spectō* _____
28. _____ *sub* _____
29. _____ *tamen* _____
30. _____ *ūnus* _____
31. _____ *ut* _____

PYRAMUS AND THISBE
METAMORPHOSES 4.55-92

55 "Pyramus et Thisbe, iuvenum pulcherrimus alter,
altera, quas Oriens habuit, praelata puellis,
contiguas tenuere domos, ubi dicitur altam
coctilibus muris cinxisse Semiramis urbem.
notitiam primosque gradus vicinia fecit,
60 tempore crevit amor; taedae quoque iure coissent,
sed vetuere patres; quod non potuere vetare,
ex aequo captis ardebant mentibus ambo.
conscius omnis abest, nutu signisque loquuntur,
quoque magis tegitur, tectus magis aestuat ignis.
65 fissus erat tenui rima, quam duxerat olim,
cum fieret, paries domui communis utrique.
id vitium nulli per saecula longa notatum—
quid non sentit amor?—primi vidistis amantes
et vocis fecistis iter, tutaeque per illud
70 murmure blanditiae minimo transire solebant.
saepe, ubi constiterant hinc Thisbe, Pyramus illinc,
inque vices fuerat captatus anhelitus oris,
'invide' dicebant 'paries, quid amantibus obstas?
quantum erat, ut sineres toto nos corpore iungi,
75 aut, hoc si nimium est, vel ad oscula danda pateres?
nec sumus ingrati: tibi nos debere fatemur,
quod datus est verbis ad amicas transitus auris.'
talia diversa nequiquam sede locuti
sub noctem dixere 'vale' partique dedere
80 oscula quisque suae non pervenientia contra.
postera nocturnos Aurora removerat ignes,
solque pruinosas radiis siccaverat herbas:
ad solitum coiere locum. tum murmure parvo
multa prius questi statuunt, ut nocte silenti
85 fallere custodes foribusque excedere temptent,
cumque domo exierint, urbis quoque tecta relinquant,
neve sit errandum lato spatiantibus arvo,
conveniant ad busta Nini lateantque sub umbra
arboris: arbor ibi niveis uberrima pomis,
90 ardua morus, erat, gelido contermina fonti.
pacta placent; et lux, tarde discedere visa,
praecipitatur aquis, et aquis nox exit ab isdem.

Short Answer Questions

Line 56 — What is the form of *praelata*? _____

What is its first principal part? _____

What word does *praelata* modify? _____

Line 58 — What is the case and use of *coctilibus muris*? _____

Line 65 — What is the form of *fissus*? _____

What word does *fissus* modify? _____

Line 66 — What is the mood and reason for *fieret*? _____

What is the case and use of *domui*? _____

Line 68 — What is the form of *amantes*? _____

What word does *amantes* modify? _____

Line 69 — What is the case and use of *vocis*? _____

Line 74 — What is the mood and reason for *sineres*? _____

What is the form of *iungi*? _____

How is this form used? _____

Line 80 — What is the form of *pervenientia*? _____

What does *pervenientia* modify? _____

Line 82 — What is the case and use of *radiis*? _____

Line 83 — What is the form of *coiere*? _____

Line 86 — What is the case and use of *domo*? _____

What is the form of *exierint*? _____

How is this form used? _____

Line 88 — What is the form of *conveniant*? _____

Multiple Choice Questions *Suggested time: 12 minutes*

1. The antecedent to *quas* in line 56 is
   a. *altera* (line 56)
   b. *Oriens* (line 56)
   c. *puellis* (line 56)
   d. *Thisbe* (line 55)

2. The metrical pattern of the first four feet of line 58 is
   a. spondee-dactyl-spondee-dactyl
   b. dactyl-spondee-spondee-dactyl
   c. dactyl-spondee-dactyl-spondee
   d. dactyl-dactyl-spondee-spondee

3. What figure of speech is employed in line 64?
   a. hyperbaton
   b. irony
   c. anaphora
   d. polyptoton

4. Whom is the poet addressing in line 68, *quid non sentit amor?*
   a. the lovers
   b. their parents
   c. the wall
   d. his general audience

5. In line 81, *nocturnos . . . ignes* are
   a. stars
   b. campfires
   c. the fires of love
   d. hearth fires

6. In line 85, the *custodes* are
   a. guards
   b. servants
   c. parents
   d. all of the above

7. *tecta*, in line 86, is an example of
   a. metonymy
   b. synecdoche
   c. personification
   d. simile

8. In line 87, *neve sit errrandum . . . spatiantibus*, is best translated
   a. so that they should not make a mistake while wandering
   b. so that there would not be a wandering about for those walking
   c. so that it must not be wandered by those walking about
   d. so that they did not walk about wandering.

9. *conveniant* in line 88 is a subjunctive in a
   a. purpose clause
   b. consecutive clause
   c. relative clause of characteristic
   d. temporal clause

10. The best translation for line 92 (*praecipitatur . . . isdem*) is
   a. it (the light) sinks into the waters, and night goes out from the same waters
   b. it (the light) sunk into the water, and the night exits from the same water
   c. it (the light) dives into waters, and the waters come out in the same night
   d. the sun goes down, into the water, and night comes up all the same

Translation *Suggested time: 15 minutes*

Translate the passage below as literally as possible.

>"Pyramus et Thisbe, iuvenum pulcherrimus alter,
>altera, quas Oriens habuit, praelata puellis,
>contiguas tenuere domos, ubi dicitur altam
>coctilibus muris cinxisse Semiramis urbem.
>5 notitiam primosque gradus vicinia fecit,
>tempore crevit amor; taedae quoque iure coissent,
>sed vetuere patres; quod non potuere vetare,
>ex aequo captis ardebant mentibus ambo.

Short Analysis Questions

1. a. Lines 69–70 contain an example of what figure of speech?

   _____

   b. Why is this figure particularly appropriate for the situation of Pyramus and Thisbe?

   _____

2. Briefly describe the effect of the direct address in lines 73–77.

   _____

   _____

3. a. Write out a literal translation of *conveniant ad busta Nini, lateantque sub umbra/arboris* (lines 88–89).

   _____

   _____

   b. Comment on how these lines foreshadow the outcome of the lovers' plan

   _____

   _____

   _____

   _____

PYRAMUS AND THISBE
METAMORPHOSES 4.93–127

"Callida per tenebras versato cardine Thisbe
egreditur fallitque suos adopertaque vultum
95 pervenit ad tumulum dictaque sub arbore sedit
audacem faciebat amor. venit ecce recenti
caede leaena boum spumantis oblita rictus,
depositura sitim vicini fontis in unda;
quam procul ad lunae radios Babylonia Thisbe
100 vidit et obscurum timido pede fugit in antrum,
dumque fugit, tergo velamina lapsa reliquit.
ut lea saeva sitim multa conpescuit unda,
dum redit in silvas, inventos forte sine ipsa
ore cruentato tenues laniavit amictus.
105 serius egressus vestigia vidit in alto
pulvere certa ferae totoque expalluit ore
Pyramus; ut vero vestem quoque sanguine tinctam
repperit, 'una duos' inquit 'nox perdet amantes,
e quibus illa fuit longa dignissima vita;
110 nostra nocens anima est. ego te, miseranda, peremi,
in loca plena metus qui iussi nocte venires
nec prior huc veni. nostrum divellite corpus
et scelerata fero consumite viscera morsu,
o quicumque sub hac habitatis rupe leones!
115 sed timidi est optare necem.' velamina Thisbes
tollit et ad pactae secum fert arboris umbram,
utque dedit notae lacrimas, dedit oscula vesti,
'accipe nunc' inquit 'nostri quoque sanguinis haustus!'
quoque erat accinctus, demisit in ilia ferrum,
120 nec mora, ferventi moriens e vulnere traxit.
ut iacuit resupinus humo, cruor emicat alte,
non aliter quam cum vitiato fistula plumbo
scinditur et tenui stridente foramine longas
eiaculatur aquas atque ictibus aera rumpit.
125 arborei fetus adspergine caedis in atram
vertuntur faciem, madefactaque sanguine radix
purpureo tinguit pendentia mora colore.

Short Answer Questions

Line 93	What is the case and use of *versato cardine*? _____
Line 94	What is the case and use of *vultum*? _____
Line 97	What is the case of *oblita*? _____
	What word does *oblita* modify? _____
	What is the case and use of *rictus*? _____
Line 101	What is the case and number of *lapsa*? _____
	What word does *lapsa* modify? _____
Line 103	Translate *sine ipsa*. _____
	Although commonly thought of as an adverb, *forte* is actually the ablative form of which noun? _____
Line 110	What is the case of *miseranda*? _____
Line 111	What is the form of *venires*? _____
	How is this form used? _____
Line 115	What is the form of *optare*? _____
	How is this form used? _____
Line 118	What is the form of *accipe*? _____
	Whom is Pyramus addressing? _____
Line 120	What is the form of *moriens*? _____
	What does *moriens* modify? _____
Line 121	What is the case and use of *humo*? _____

Multiple Choice Questions *Suggested time: 12 minutes*

1. Line 95 (*pervenit . . . sedit*) is best translated as
   a. she arrives at the appointed tomb and sits under a tree
   b. she comes to the tomb and the tree having been appointed, she sits
   c. she arrives at the tomb and sits under the appointed tree
   d. the tomb having been appointed, she sits under the tree

2. In lines 96–97, we learn that
   a. a lion has a bloody mouth from a recent kill
   b. a lioness arrives, her mouth besmeared with blood from a recent kill of cattle
   c. there has been a recent slaughter of a lioness near the tomb
   d. a lioness arrives famished at the tomb of Ninus

3. What figure of speech is used in line 100?
   a. transferred epithet
   b. hyperbaton
   c. litotes
   d. hyperbole

4. How does the position of *Pyramus* in lines 105–107 at the end of the clause contribute to the meaning of the lines?
   a. it shows how important he is as a lover
   b. it reinforces the fact that he is late
   c. it emphasizes his pallor
   d. it heightens suspense

5. What is the metrical pattern for the first four feet of line 108?
   a. dactyl-spondee-dactyl-spondee
   b. spondee-dactyl-spondee-dactyl
   c. spondee-spondee-dactyl-spondee
   d. dactyl-dactyl-spondee-spondee

6. How does the word order in line 108 reinforce the line's meaning?
   a. it shows how quickly one's fortunes can change
   b. it emphasizes that there were two lovers
   c. it interlocks the fate of the two lovers
   d. it shows the power of night

7. Whom is Pyramus addressing in line 112?
   a. *custodes* (line 85)
   b. Thisbe
   c. any lions in the cave
   d. the lioness

8. Why does Pyramus call his *viscera scelerata* in line 113?
   a. because he feels guilty for coming too late
   b. because he thinks Thisbe is dead
   c. because he deceived his parents
   d. because he wants the lions to eat him

9. The metrical pattern of the first four feet of line 121 is
   a. dactyl-spondee-dactyl-dactyl
   b. dactyl-spondee-spondee-dactyl
   c. dactyl-dactyl-dactyl-dactyl
   d. spondee-spondee-dactyl-dactyl

10. Lines 125–127 describe
    a. the death of Pyramus
    b. the death of the mulberry tree
    c. the color of Pyramus' blood
    d. the cause of the mulberries' dark color

Translation *Suggested time: 15 minutes*

Translate the passage below as literally as possible.

>   ut lea saeva sitim multa conpescuit unda,
>   dum redit in silvas, inventos forte sine ipsa
>   ore cruentato tenues laniavit amictus.
>   serius egressus vestigia vidit in alto
> 5   pulvere certa ferae totoque expalluit ore
>   Pyramus; ut vero vestem quoque sanguine tinctam
>   repperit, 'una duos' inquit 'nox perdet amantes,
>   e quibus illa fuit longa dignissima vita;

Short Analysis Questions

1. a. Translate *nostra nocens anima est/ ego te, miseranda, peremi* (line 110).

   b. What is the effect of the juxtaposition of the words *ego te* (line 110)?

   c. What is the effect of the apostrophe *miseranda* (line 110)?

2. a. Translate *sed timidi est optare necem* (line 115).

   b. Explain what this typical Roman maxim means in the context of this passage.

3. a. To what does the poet compare Pyramus' wound in lines 122–124?

   b. Which figure of speech does this simile employ?

4. Lines 125–127 describe a metamorphosis.

   a. What is transformed? _____

   b. What was the original color of the fruit? _____

PYRAMUS AND THISBE
METAMORPHOSES 4.128–166

"Ecce metu nondum posito, ne fallat amantem,
illa redit iuvenemque oculis animoque requirit,
130 quantaque vitarit narrare pericula gestit;
utque locum et visa cognoscit in arbore formam,
sic facit incertam pomi color: haeret, an haec sit.
dum dubitat, tremebunda videt pulsare cruentum
membra solum, retroque pedem tulit, oraque buxo
135 pallidiora gerens exhorruit aequoris instar,
quod tremit, exigua cum summum stringitur aura.
sed postquam remorata suos cognovit amores,
percutit indignos claro plangore lacertos
et laniata comas amplexaque corpus amatum
140 vulnera supplevit lacrimis fletumque cruori
miscuit et gelidis in vultibus oscula figens
'Pyrame,' clamavit, 'quis te mihi casus ademit?
Pyrame, responde! tua te carissima Thisbe
nominat; exaudi vultusque attolle iacentes!'
145 ad nomen Thisbes oculos a morte gravatos
Pyramus erexit visaque recondidit illa.

"Quae postquam vestemque suam cognovit et ense
vidit ebur vacuum, 'tua te manus' inquit 'amorque
perdidit, infelix! est et mihi fortis in unum
150 hoc manus, est et amor: dabit hic in vulnera vires.
persequar extinctum letique miserrima dicar
causa comesque tui: quique a me morte revelli
heu sola poteras, poteris nec morte revelli.
hoc tamen amborum verbis estote rogati,
155 o multum miseri meus illiusque parentes,
ut, quos certus amor, quos hora novissima iunxit,
conponi tumulo non invideatis eodem;
at tu, quae ramis arbor miserabile corpus
nunc tegis unius, mox es tectura duorum,
160 signa tene caedis pullosque et luctibus aptos
semper habe fetus, gemini monimenta cruoris.'
dixit et aptato pectus mucrone sub imum
incubuit ferro, quod adhuc a caede tepebat.
vota tamen tetigere deos, tetigere parentes:
165 nam color in pomo est, ubi permaturuit, ater,
quodque rogis superest, una requiescit in urna."

PYRAMUS AND THISBE: METAMORPHOSES 4.128–166 • 79

Short Answer Questions

Line 128   What is the construction of *metu nondum posito*? _____

Translate the construction. _____

What is the form of *fallat*? _____

How is this form used? _____

Line 129   What is the case and use of *oculis*? _____

Line 130   What is the form of *vitarit*? _____

How is this form used? _____

Line 131   What is the form of *visa*? _____

Translate *visa*. _____

Line 135   What is the case and use of *aequoris*? _____

Line 139   What is the form of *laniata*? _____

What word does *laniata* modify? _____

Translate *laniata*. _____

What is the case and use of *comas*? _____

Line 140   What is the case and use of *cruori*? _____

Line 145   What is the case and use of *morte*? _____

Line 152   What is the form of *revelli*? _____

How is this form used? _____

Line 157   What is the form of *invideatis*? _____

How is this form used? _____

Multiple Choice Questions *Suggested time: 12 minutes*

1. In line 129, *oculis animoque requirit* is an example of which figure of speech?
   - a. hyperbole
   - b. hendiadys
   - c. zeugma
   - d. hysteron proteron

2. The metrical pattern of the first four feet of line 132 is
   - a. dactyl-dactyl-spondee-spondee
   - b. dactyl-spondee-dactyl-spondee
   - c. dactyl-spondee-spondee-dactyl
   - d. spondee-dactyl-spondee-dactyl

3. In lines 132–134, Thisbe becomes fearful because
   a. she isn't sure she is in the right place
   b. she sees that the color of the berries has changed
   c. she sees Pyramus' trembling limbs beating the ground
   d. all of the above

4. *buxo* in line 134 is an ablative of
   a. means
   b. manner
   c. agent
   d. comparison

5. In line 138, *indignos . . . lacertos* is an example of
   a. a metaphor
   b. a simile
   c. hyperbole
   d. personification

6. Line 142 (*'Pyrame,' . . . ademit?*) is best translated
   a. Pyramus called, who has taken away from me your accident?
   b. Pyramus, she called, what accident has taken you from me?
   c. Pyramus, she called, who has taken you from me by accident?
   d. Pryamus shouted who has taken you away from me?

7. In lines 149–150, we learn that Thisbe
   a. has a brave hand
   b. has brave love
   c. has decided to kill herself
   d. is strong

8. The case of *sola* (line 153) is
   a. nominative singular
   b. neuter plural
   c. vocative singular
   d. ablative singular

9. In line 157, Thisbe addresses
   a. Pyramus
   b. their fathers
   c. the tree
   d. the tomb

10. The antecedent to *quod* (line 166) is
    a. *ater* (line 165)
    b. *color* (line 165)
    c. *id* (understood)
    d. *pomo* (line 165)

Translation *Suggested time: 15 minutes*

Translate the passage below as literally as possible.

> o multum miseri meus illiusque parentes,
> ut, quos certus amor, quos hora novissima iunxit,
> conponi tumulo non invideatis eodem;
> at tu, quae ramis arbor miserabile corpus
> 5   nunc tegis unius, mox es tectura duorum,
> signa tene caedis pullosque et luctibus aptos
> semper habe fetus, gemini monimenta cruoris.'

Short Analysis Questions

1. a. Translate *quantaque vitarit narrare pericula gestit* (line 130).

    b. Why is this line both pathetic and ironic?

2. a. To what does Ovid compare Thisbe's shudder in lines 135–136?

    b. How appropriate is this simile as a way of illustrating Thisbe's fear and horror?

3. In lines 138–141, Ovid describes Thisbe's gestures of mourning. Delineate six ways that Thisbe mourns. Give the Latin for each action and translate it loosely.

a. _____

b. _____

c. _____

d. _____

e. _____

f. _____

Essay *Suggested time: 20 minutes*

Pyramus and Thisbe is a tragic love story. In lines 110–112, Pyramus blames himself for Thisbe's death. Yet, the poet suggests other reasons for the tragic outcome. Write an essay in which you discuss what you believe are the major causes of the tragedy.

Support your assertions with references drawn from **throughout** lines 55–166. All Latin words must be copied or their line numbers provided, AND they must be translated or paraphrased closely enough so that it is clear you understand the Latin. It is your responsibility to convince your reader that you are basing your conclusions on the Latin text and not merely on a general recollection of the passage. Direct your answer to the question; do not merely summarize the passage. Please write your essay on a separate piece of paper.

Scansion

Scan the following lines.

dum dubitat, tremebunda videt pulsare cruentum

membra solum, retroque pedem tulit, oraque buxo

pallidiora gerens exhorruit aequoris instar,

quod tremit, exigua cum summum stringitur aura.

Vocabulary

1. Give the positive and comparative forms for *pulcherrimus* (line 55) and the meanings for each.

   a. _____   _____

   b. _____   _____

2. Give the principal parts for the verb from which *crevit* (line 60) is formed. Provide the meaning for each part.

   a. _____   _____

   b. _____   _____

   c. _____   _____

   d. _____   _____

3. Give the nominative and genitive singular, gender, and meaning for *iure* (line 60).

   _____

4. Give the principal parts and meaning for the verb from which *loquuntur* (line 63) is formed.

   a. _____   _____

   b. _____   _____

   c. _____   _____

5. Give the positive and superlative forms and meanings for *magis* (line 64).

   a. _____   _____

   b. _____   _____

6. Give the nominative singular forms for *utrique* (line 66). Give the English for this pronoun.

   a. _____   _____   _____

   b. _____

7. Give the genitive, gender, and meaning for *paries* (line 66).

   _____

8. Give the principal parts and meanings for the verb *constiterant* (line 71).

   a. _____   _____

   b. _____   _____

   c. _____   _____

84 • OVID

9. Give the nominative singular form and meaning for *amantibus* (line 73).

   _____

10. a. Write out the four principal parts of the verb *eo*.

    _____ _____ _____ _____

    b. Find all the compounds of *eo* in the *Pyramus and Thisbe* episode. Give the Latin verb form and meaning for each and provide line references in parentheses for your Latin choices.

    1. _____

    2. _____

    3. _____

    4. _____

    5. _____

    6. _____

DAEDALUS AND ICARUS
METAMORPHOSES 8.183-235

      Daedalus interea Creten longumque perosus
exilium tactusque loci natalis amore
185   clausus erat pelago. "terras licet" inquit "et undas
obstruat: et caelum certe patet; ibimus illac:
omnia possideat, non possidet aera Minos."
dixit et ignotas animum dimittit in artes
naturamque novat. nam ponit in ordine pennas
190   a minima coeptas, longam breviore sequenti,
ut clivo crevisse putes: sic rustica quondam
fistula disparibus paulatim surgit avenis;
tum lino medias et ceris alligat imas
atque ita conpositas parvo curvamine flectit,
195   ut veras imitetur aves. puer Icarus una
stabat et, ignarus sua se tractare pericla,
ore renidenti modo, quas vaga moverat aura,
captabat plumas, flavam modo pollice ceram
mollibat lusuque suo mirabile patris
200   impediebat opus. postquam manus ultima coepto
inposita est, geminas opifex libravit in alas
ipse suum corpus motaque pependit in aura;
instruit et natum "medio" que "ut limite curras,
Icare," ait "moneo, ne, si demissior ibis,
205   unda gravet pennas, si celsior, ignis adurat:
inter utrumque vola. nec te spectare Booten
aut Helicen iubeo strictumque Orionis ensem:
me duce carpe viam!" pariter praecepta volandi
tradit et ignotas umeris accommodat alas.
210   inter opus monitusque genae maduere seniles,
et patriae tremuere manus; dedit oscula nato
non iterum repetenda suo pennisque levatus
ante volat comitique timet, velut ales, ab alto
quae teneram prolem produxit in aera nido,
215   hortaturque sequi damnosasque erudit artes
et movet ipse suas et nati respicit alas.
hos aliquis tremula dum captat harundine pisces,
aut pastor baculo stivave innixus arator
vidit et obstipuit, quique aethera carpere possent,
220   credidit esse deos. et iam Iunonia laeva

parte Samos (fuerant Delosque Parosque relictae)
dextra Lebinthos erat fecundaque melle Calymne,
cum puer audaci coepit gaudere volatu
deseruitque ducem caelique cupidine tractus
225 altius egit iter. rapidi vicinia solis
mollit odoratas, pennarum vincula, ceras;
tabuerant cerae: nudos quatit ille lacertos,
remigioque carens non ullas percipit auras,
oraque caerulea patrium clamantia nomen
230 excipiuntur aqua, quae nomen traxit ab illo.
at pater infelix, nec iam pater, "Icare," dixit,
"Icare," dixit "ubi es? qua te regione requiram?"
"Icare," dicebat: pennas adspexit in undis
devovitque suas artes corpusque sepulcro
235 condidit, et tellus a nomine dicta sepulti.

Short Answer Questions

Line 185 What is the case and use of *pelago*? _____

Line 190 What is the form of *coeptas*? _____

What word does it modify? _____

Translate *coeptas*. _____

What form of the verb is *sequenti*? _____

What are the principal parts of this verb? _____
_____

Translate *breviore sequenti*. _____

What is the case and use of *sequenti*? _____

Line 191 What is the form of *putes*? _____

How is this form used? _____

Line 194 What is the case and use of *curvamine*? _____

Line 196 What is the reason for the form *tractare*? _____

What is the subject of *tractare*? _____

Line 199 What word does *mirabile* modify? _____

What case is *mirabile*? _____

Line 203   What is the form of *curras*? _____

How is this form used? _____

Line 206   What is the form of *spectare*? _____

How is this form used? _____

Line 209   What is the case and use of *umeris*? _____

Line 211   What is the case and use of *nato*? _____

Line 212   What is the form of *repetenda*? _____

What word does *repetenda* modify? _____

Translate *repetenda*. _____

Line 218   What is the case and use of *baculo*? _____

Line 224   What is the form of *tractus*? _____

What word does *tractus* modify? _____

Line 229   What is the form of *clamantia*? _____

What is the number and case of *clamantia*? _____

What word does *clamantia* modify? _____

Multiple Choice Questions *Suggested time: 12 minutes*

1. The metrical pattern for the first four feet of line 183 is
   a. dactyl-spondee-dactyl-spondee
   b. dactyl-dactyl-spondee-spondee
   c. spondee-dactyl-spondee-dactyl
   d. spondee-dactyl-dactyl-spondee

2. Line 187 (*omnia . . . Minos*) is best translated as
   a. he possesses omens, Minos does not possess the air
   b. let Minos possess all things, he does not possess the air
   c. all things possess Minos, the air does not possess Minos
   d. let all things own Minos, he does not own the air

3. Line 189 contains which figure of speech?
   a. onomatopoeia
   b. asyndeton
   c. alliteration
   d. hyperbole

4. In line 208, *me duce* is an
   a. ablative of personal agent
   b. ablative of manner
   c. ablative absolute
   d. ablative of separation

5. The figure of speech expressed by *movet ipse suas* (line 216) is
   a. irony
   b. hyperbole
   c. ellipsis
   d. hendiadys

6. In lines 217–220, the observers believe that Daedalus and Icarus are gods because
   a. they are afraid
   b. they are amazed
   c. they can fly
   d. they can seize the air

7. The antecedent of *quae* (line 230) is
   a. *ora* (line 229)
   b. *nomen* (line 230)
   c. *aqua* (line 230)
   d. *caerulea* (line 229)

8. Lines 229–230 contain both a double chiasmus and interlocked word order (synchesis). The effect of these figures is
   a. division between father and son
   b. the depiction of the love between father and son
   c. a mirroring of Icarus' fateful spiraling fall
   d. creation of an image of sea waves

9. What use of the ablative is *sepulcro* (line 234)?
   a. means
   b. manner
   c. place where
   d. agent

10. In lines 229 and 235, the poet provides two examples of *aitia* based on the name of
    a. Daedalus
    b. the ocean
    c. an island
    d. Icarus

Translation *Suggested time: 15 minutes*

Translate the passage below as literally as possible.

> dixit et ignotas animum dimittit in artes
> naturamque novat. nam ponit in ordine pennas
> a minima coeptas, longam breviore sequenti,
> ut clivo crevisse putes: sic rustica quondam
> 5   fistula disparibus paulatim surgit avenis;
> tum lino medias et ceris alligat imas
> atque ita conpositas parvo curvamine flectit,
> ut veras imitetur aves.

Short Analysis Questions

1. List two ways in which Icarus hinders his father's work (lines 195–200). Be sure to use Latin words in your answer.

    a. _____

    b. _____

    c. What is Icarus's state of mind in this passage? Again, use Latin words as examples in your response.

2. What four instructions does Daedalus give to Icarus? Use Latin words in your response.

   a. _____

   b. _____

   c. _____

   d. _____

3. Why does the poet call the wings *ignotas* in line 209?

   _____
   _____
   _____

4. a. Translate *velut ales, ab alto/ quae teneram prolem produxit in aera nido,/ horaturque sequi* (lines 213–215).

   _____

   b. Briefly explain the appropriateness of this simile.

   _____
   _____
   _____
   _____

Essay *Suggested time: 20 minutes*

The story of Daedalus and Icarus illustrates the ancient maxim, "nothing in excess," carved on the temple of Apollo at Delphi. Write an essay in which you discuss how the actions of both father and son are illustrative of the importance of this maxim.

Support your assertions with references drawn from **throughout** the passage. All Latin words must be copied or their line numbers provided, AND they must be translated or paraphrased closely enough so that it is clear you understand the Latin. It is your responsibility to convince your reader that you are basing your conclusions on the Latin text and not merely on a general recollection of the passage. Direct your answer to the question; do not merely summarize the passage. Please write your essay on a separate piece of paper.

Scansion

Scan the following lines.

at pater infelix, nec iam pater, "Icare," dixit

"Icare," dixit, "ubi es? qua te regione requiram?"

"Icare," dicebat: pennas adspexit in undis

devovitque suas artes corpusque sepulcro

Vocabulary

1. List all the nouns for birds, feathers, and flight. Provide the dictionary entry and the meaning for each word. Provide line references in parentheses beside each Latin word you list.

   a. _____
   b. _____
   c. _____
   d. _____
   e. _____
   f. _____
   g. _____
   h. _____
   i. _____
   j. _____
   k. _____

2. List all the principal parts and meaning for all verbs that refer to movement of the body or to flight. Provide line references in parentheses beside each Latin word you list.

a. _____

b. _____

c. _____

d. _____

e. _____

f. _____

g. _____

h. _____

i. _____

j. _____

k. _____

l. _____

PHILEMON AND BAUCIS
METAMORPHOSES 8.616–650

obstipuere omnes nec talia dicta probarunt,
ante omnesque Lelex animo maturus et aevo,
sic ait: "inmensa est finemque potentia caeli
non habet, et quicquid superi voluere, peractum est,
620 quoque minus dubites, tiliae contermina quercus
collibus est Phrygiis modico circumdata muro;
ipse locum vidi; nam me Pelopeia Pittheus
misit in arva suo quondam regnata parenti.
haud procul hinc stagnum est, tellus habitabilis olim,
625 nunc celebres mergis fulicisque palustribus undae;
Iuppiter huc specie mortali cumque parente
venit Atlantiades positis caducifer alis.
mille domos adiere locum requiemque petentes,
mille domos clausere serae; tamen una recepit,
630 parva quidem, stipulis et canna tecta palustri,
sed pia Baucis anus parilique aetate Philemon
illa sunt annis iuncti iuvenalibus, illa
consenuere casa paupertatemque fatendo
effecere levem nec iniqua mente ferendo;
635 nec refert, dominos illic famulosne requiras:
tota domus duo sunt, idem parentque iubentque.
ergo ubi caelicolae parvos tetigere penates
summissoque humiles intrarunt vertice postes,
membra senex posito iussit relevare sedili;
640 cui superiniecit textum rude sedula Baucis
inque foco tepidum cinerem dimovit et ignes
suscitat hesternos foliisque et cortice sicco
nutrit et ad flammas anima producit anili
multifidasque faces ramaliaque arida tecto
645 detulit et minuit parvoque admovit aeno,
quodque suus coniunx riguo conlegerat horto,
truncat holus foliis; furca levat ille bicorni
sordida terga suis nigro pendentia tigno
servatoque diu resecat de tergore partem
650 exiguam sectamque domat ferventibus undis.

Short Answer Questions

Line 616	What is the form of *obstipuere*?	
Line 617	What is the case and use of the two words *animo . . . aevo*?	
Lines 618–619	What subject do *est* (618) and *habet* (619) share?	
Line 619	With which word does *peractum* agree?	
Line 620	What two words agree with *quercus*?	
Line 625	What word does *celebres* modify?	
Line 628	What is the subject of *adiere*?	
Line 629	What is the subject of *clausere*?	
	What noun does *una* modify?	
Line 631	What type of ablative is *parilique aetate*?	
Line 634	What noun does *levem* modify?	
Line 639	What is the missing subject for *relevare*?	

Lines 641–647 What is the subject for *dimovit* (line 641), *suscitat* (line 642), *nutrit* (line 643), *producit* (line 643), *detulit* (line 645), *minuit* (line 645), *admovit* (line 645), and *truncat* (line 647)?

Line 647 What is the subject of *levat*?

Multiple Choice Questions *Suggested time: 12 minutes*

1. According to Lelex, in lines 618–619,
   a. he does not believe the gods are all powerful
   b. the gods are all powerful
   c. the gods do not have great power
   d. the gods do not dwell in heaven

2. The best translation for *tiliae contermina quercus* (line 620) is
   a. a linden tree's oak nearby
   b. an oak adjacent to a linden tree
   c. an oak and a linden tree nearby
   d. a linden tree adjacent to an oak

3. Which of the following figures of speech can be found in line 625 (*nunc . . . undae*)?
   a. hyperbaton
   b. alliteration
   c. chiasmus
   d. synchesis

96 • OVID

4. To whom is *Atlantiades* (line 627) a reference?
   a. Atlas
   b. Jupiter
   c. Mercury
   d. Atalanta

5. The best translation for the phrase *mille domos clausere serae* (line 629) is
   a. a thousand homes closed their crossbars
   b. a thousand crossbars closed their homes
   c. the houses closed a thousand crossbars
   d. crossbars closed the homes a thousand times

6. What is the case and number of both *illa* and *illa* in line 632?
   a. nominative singular
   b. ablative singular
   c. nominative plural
   d. accusative plural

7. The best translation for *paupertatemque . . . ferendo* (lines 633–34) is
   a. they made their poverty light and not resentful by professing it and bearing it
   b. they bore their poverty with a not resentful mind and made it light by professing it
   c. they professed their poverty and bore it with a not resentful mind making it light
   d. by professing their poverty and by bearing it with a not resentful mind they made it light

8. The metrical pattern of the first four feet of line 644 is
   a. dactyl-dactyl-dactyl-dactyl
   b. dactyl-dactyl-spondee-spondee
   c. dactyl-spondee-dactyl-dactyl
   d. dactyl-dactyl-spondee-dactyl

9. Lines 646–647 contain an example of
   a. assonance
   b. a golden line
   c. synchesis
   d. prolepsis

10. In lines 647–650, we learn that
    a. the vegetables are prepared
    b. the couch is prepared
    c. the meat is prepared
    d. the fire is prepared

Translation *Suggested time: 15 minutes*

Translate the passage below as literally as possible.

"inmensa est finemque potentia caeli
non habet, et quicquid superi voluere, peractum est,
quoque minus dubites, tiliae contermina quercus
collibus est Phrygiis modico circumdata muro;
5   ipse locum vidi; nam me Pelopeia Pittheus
misit in arva suo quondam regnata parenti.

Short Analysis Questions

1. How does the embracing word order of line 621, *modico circumdata muro*, reinforce the meaning of the phrase?

2. Line 637 (*ergo . . . penates*) contains a metonymy. Write out the Latin that expresses the metonymy and explain why it qualifies as a metonymy.

3. In lines 641–645 (*inque . . . detulit*), we are given a **very** detailed account of how Baucis prepares the fire. Write out three Latin nouns and adjective phrases that describe the materials Baucis used in her preparation. Translate each of your choices.

Vocabulary

Below you will find a list of high frequency words you have encountered in your recent readings. For all the words you know, write out full dictionary entries, including English meanings, and put a √ mark in the left-hand column to show you have already committed these words to memory. For any words you do not yet know, write out the dictionary entries using the end glossary and learn them as soon as possible.

√

1. ____ *aiō* _____
2. ____ *āla* _____
3. ____ *amans* _____
4. ____ *aqua* _____
5. ____ *caelum* _____
6. ____ *captō* _____
7. ____ *cingō* _____
8. ____ *coniunx* _____
9. ____ *corpus* _____
10. ____ *crescō* _____
11. ____ *cum* preposition _____
12. ____ *cum* conjunction _____
13. ____ *custōs* _____
14. ____ *domus* _____
15. ____ *dum* _____
16. ____ *duo* _____
17. ____ *fallō* _____
18. ____ *ferō* _____
19. ____ *fīō* _____
20. ____ *foris* _____
21. ____ *ignis* _____

22. ____ *iubeō* _____

23. ____ *iuvenis* _____

24. ____ *locus* _____

25. ____ *loquor* _____

26. ____ *nē* _____

27. ____ *pars* _____

28. ____ *parvus* _____

29. ____ *pōnō* _____

30. ____ *tellus* _____

31. ____ *ubi* _____

32. ____ *unda* _____

PHILEMON AND BAUCIS
METAMORPHOSES 8.651–678

651* interea medias fallunt sermonibus horas
655 concutiuntque torum de molli fluminis ulva
     inpositum lecto sponda pedibusque salignis.
     vestibus hunc velant, quas non nisi tempore festo
     sternere consuerant, sed et haec vilisque vetusque
     vestis erat, lecto non indignanda saligno.
660 adcubuere dei. mensam succincta tremensque
     ponit anus, mensae sed erat pes tertius inpar:
     testa parem fecit; quae postquam subdita clivum
     sustulit, aequatam mentae tersere virentes.
     ponitur hic bicolor sincerae baca Minervae
665 conditaque in liquida corna autumnalia faece
     intibaque et radix et lactis massa coacti
     ovaque non acri leviter versata favilla,
     omnia fictilibus. post haec caelatus eodem
     sistitur argento crater fabricataque fago
670 pocula, qua cava sunt, flaventibus inlita ceris;
     parva mora est, epulasque foci misere calentes,
     nec longae rursus referuntur vina senectae
     dantque locum mensis paulum seducta secundis:
     hic nux, hic mixta est rugosis carica palmis
675 prunaque et in patulis redolentia mala canistris
     et de purpureis conlectae vitibus uvae,
     candidus in medio favus est; super omnia vultus
     accessere boni nec iners pauperque voluntas.

Short Answer Questions

Line 657   What is the antecedent of *quas?* _____

Line 660   What is the form of *adcubuere?* _____

            Which noun does *succincta* modify? _____

Line 661   On which noun is the genitive *mensae* dependent? _____

Line 663   What is the subject of *tersere?* _____

* Four lines, 652–655a, are of questionable authenticity and are omitted from this text.

Line 664 What are all the subjects of *ponitur*? Provide line references in parentheses for your Latin choices.

_____

_____

_____

Line 668 What word does *caelatus* modify? _____

Line 678 What are all the subjects of *accessere*? _____

Multiple Choice Questions *Suggested time: 10 minutes*

1. With what noun does *indignanda* (line 659) agree?
   a. *anus* (line 661)
   b. *vestis* (line 659)
   c. *sponda* (line 656)
   d. *mensam* (line 660)

2. *non indignanda* (line 659) is an example of
   a. chiasmus
   b. irony
   c. alliteration
   d. litotes

3. What is the antecedent of *quae* (line 662)?
   a. *testa* (line 662)
   b. *pes* (line 661)
   c. *clivum* (line 662)
   d. *mensae* (line 661)

4. The best translation for line 667 (*ovaque . . . favilla*) is
   a. eggs turned lightly not in warm ashes
   b. eggs turned lightly in warm ashes
   c. not eggs turned lightly in warm ashes
   d. eggs not turned lightly in warm ashes

5. From line 672 (*nec longae . . . senectae*), we learn that
   a. well-aged wines are drunk
   b. the old man and woman bring out country wines
   c. young wine is drunk throughout the meal
   d. no wine is drunk during the meal

6. The best translation for line 674 (*hic . . . palmis*) is
   a. here a nut, here wrinkly date mixed with figs
   b. this nut, this fig mixed with wrinkly date
   c. here a nut, here a fig mixed with wrinkly dates
   d. this nut, this date mixed with wrinkly fig

7. From lines 677–678 (*super . . . voluntas*), we learn that
   a. happy faces and good will abounded
   b. the faces of good people and good will abounded
   c. the faces of happy people and lazy spirits were present
   d. it is clear the guests would rather not be present

8. The metrical pattern for the first four feet of line 678 is
   a. dactyl-dactyl-spondee-spondee
   b. dactyl-spondee-spondee-dactyl
   c. dactyl-spondee-dactyl-spondee
   d. spondee-dactyl-dactyl-spondee

Translation *Suggested time: 15 minutes*

Translate the passage below as literally as possible.

> vestibus hunc velant, quas non nisi tempore festo
> sternere consuerant, sed et haec vilisque vetusque
> vestis erat, lecto non indignanda saligno.
> adcubuere dei. mensam succincta tremensque
> 5 ponit anus, mensae sed erat pes tertius inpar:
> testa parem fecit; quae postquam subdita clivum
> sustulit, aequatam mentae tersere virentes.

Short Analysis Questions

1. Write out the Latin and explain a polysyndeton and alliteration from the phrase *sed et haec vilisque vetusque / vestis erat* (lines 658–659).

2. a. Write out the Latin that expresses a chiasmus in line 665.

   b. Explain how this chiasmus reinforces the meaning of the line.

3. Explain the transferred epithet in line 676 (*et de purpureis . . . uvae*).

Vocabulary

Below you will find a list of high frequency words you have encountered in your recent readings. For all the words you know, write out full dictionary entries, including English meanings, and put a √ mark in the left-hand column to show you have already committed these words to memory. For any words you do not yet know, write out the dictionary entries using the end glossary and learn them as soon as possible.

√

1. _____ āēr _____
2. _____ altus _____
3. _____ animus _____
4. _____ caedēs _____
5. _____ cera _____
6. _____ cognoscō _____
7. _____ mollis _____
8. _____ mora _____
9. _____ mensa _____
10. _____ pōmum _____
11. _____ postquam _____
12. _____ relinquō _____
13. _____ sanguinis _____
14. _____ sentiō _____
15. _____ signum _____
16. _____ tangō _____
17. _____ tenuis _____
18. _____ timidus _____
19. _____ tingō _____
20. _____ transeō _____
21. _____ umbra _____

22. ____ *tegō*
23. ____ *veniō*
24. ____ *verbum*
25. ____ *vestigium*
26. ____ *vestis*
27. ____ *vetō*
28. ____ *volō*
29. ____ *votum*
30. ____ *vultus*

PHILEMON AND BAUCIS
METAMORPHOSES 8.679-724

"Interea totiens haustum cratera repleri
680 sponte sua per seque vident succrescere vina:
attoniti novitate pavent manibusque supinis
concipiunt Baucisque preces timidusque Philemon
et veniam dapibus nullisque paratibus orant.
unicus anser erat, minimae custodia villae:
685 quem dis hospitibus domini mactare parabant;
ille celer penna tardos aetate fatigat
eluditque diu tandemque est visus ad ipsos
confugisse deos: superi vetuere necari
'di' que 'sumus, meritasque luet vicinia poenas
690 inpia' dixerunt; 'vobis inmunibus huius
esse mali dabitur; modo vestra relinquite tecta
ac nostros comitate gradus et in ardua montis
ite simul!' parent ambo baculisque levati
nituntur longo vestigia ponere clivo.
695 tantum aberant summo, quantum semel ire sagitta
missa potest: flexere oculos et mersa palude
cetera prospiciunt, tantum sua tecta manere,
dumque ea mirantur, dum deflent fata suorum,
illa vetus, dominis etiam casa parva duobus
700 vertitur in templum: furcas subiere columnae,
stramina flavescunt aurataque tecta videntur
caelataeque fores adopertaque marmore tellus.
talia tum placido Saturnius edidit ore:
'dicite, iuste senex et femina coniuge iusto
705 digna, quid optetis.' cum Baucide pauca locutus
iudicium superis aperit commune Philemon:
'esse sacerdotes delubraque vestra tueri
poscimus, et quoniam concordes egimus annos,
auferat hora duos eadem, nec coniugis umquam
710 busta meae videam, neu sim tumulandus ab illa.'
vota fides sequitur: templi tutela fuere,
donec vita data est; annis aevoque soluti
ante gradus sacros cum starent forte locique
narrarent casus, frondere Philemona Baucis,
715 Baucida conspexit senior frondere Philemon.

```
            iamque super geminos crescente cacumine vultus
            mutua, dum licuit, reddebant dicta 'vale' que
            'o coniunx' dixere simul, simul abdita texit
            ora frutex: ostendit adhuc Thyneius illic
    720     incola de gemino vicinos corpore truncos.
            haec mihi non vani (neque erat, cur fallere vellent)
            narravere senes; equidem pendentia vidi
            serta super ramos ponensque recentia dixi
            'cura deum di sint, et, qui coluere, colantur.'"
```

Short Answer Questions

Line 679   Which noun does *haustum* modify? _____

Line 681   What case is *attoniti*? _____

           With what does it agree? _____

Line 683   What is the case and use of *dapibus nullisque paratibus*?

           _____

Lines 692–693   Of what verb form are *comitate* (line 692) and *ite* (line 693) examples?

           _____

Line 693   What is the case and use of *baculis*? _____

           On which other word in this line does it depend? _____

Line 696   What is the form of *flexere*? _____

Line 704   What case are *senex* and *femina*? _____

Line 705   What verb form is *locutus*? _____

           What are the principal parts of the verb from which *locutus* is formed?

           _____

           Which noun does *locutus* modify? _____

Lines 709–710   What three jussive subjunctive verbs form their request in these lines?

           _____

Line 712   With which words does the participle *soluti* agree? _____

           _____

Line 714   What is the subject of *frondere*? _____

Multiple Choice Questions *Suggested time: 12 minutes*

1. To whom does *superi* (line 688) refer?
   a. Philemon and Baucis
   b. Jupiter and Mercury
   c. the gods of Olympus
   d. the old people

2. What is the case and number of *gradus* (line 692)?
   a. nominative plural
   b. nominative singular
   c. genitive singular
   d. accusative plural

3. From lines 695–696, we learn that
   a. Philemon and Baucis have nearly reached the top of the mountain
   b. Philemon and Baucis have a long way to go to reach the top of the mountain
   c. Philemon and Baucis flee because they are being shot at with arrows
   d. Philemon and Baucis begin to shoot arrows at their neighbors

4. In line 703, *Saturnius* refers to
   a. Saturn
   b. Mercury
   c. Jupiter
   d. the temple

5. The best translation for lines 704–705 (*dicite . . . digna*) is
   a. tell the just man and the woman's just husband
   b. tell, just old man, worthy of a just female wife
   c. tell, just old man and woman, worthy of a just husband
   d. old man, tell your wife, worthy of a just husband

6. The best translation for line 716 (*iamque . . . vultus*) is
   a. and now with a treetop growing over their twin faces
   b. and now a treetop grows over their twin faces
   c. and now over their twin faces grows a treetop
   d. and now twin treetops grow over their faces

7. The metrical pattern of the first four feet of line 720 is
   a. dactyl-spondee-dactyl-spondee
   b. dactyl-dactyl-dactyl-spondee
   c. dactyl-spondee-spondee-spondee
   d. dactyl-dactyl-spondee-spondee

8. The figure of speech found in line 720 is
   a. synecdoche
   b. synchesis
   c. chiasmus
   d. hyperbaton

9. Who is the subject of *vidi* (line 722)?
   a. Philemon
   b. Lelex
   c. Baucis
   d. Thyneius

10. The best translation for *cura deum di sunt* (line 724) is
    a. let the gods care for those who are gods
    b. let those who are a care of the gods be gods
    c. let the gods worship those who are a care to the gods
    d. let those whom the gods worship be gods

Translation *Suggested time: 15 minutes*

Translate the passage below as literally as possible.

> tantum aberant summo, quantum semel ire sagitta
> missa potest: flexere oculos et mersa palude
> cetera prospiciunt, tantum sua tecta manere,
> dumque ea mirantur, dum deflent fata suorum,
> 5 illa vetus, dominis etiam casa parva duobus
> vertitur in templum: furcas subiere columnae,
> stramina flavescunt aurataque tecta videntur
> caelataeque fores adopertaque marmore tellus.

Short Analysis Questions

1. Explain how the meter of line 686 reinforces the meaning of the line.

2. Briefly describe, without translating word for word, what is happening in lines 684–688 (*unicus . . . deos*).

3. In describing the wine bowl filling up of its own accord, Ovid uses a striking alliteration in line 680. Write out and explain the Latin that expresses the alliteration.

Essay *Suggested time: 20 minutes*

In this story of piety and loyalty to the gods we see the magnanimous spirits of Philemon and Baucis contrasted with the poverty of their daily existence. In an essay, evaluate this story as a contrast between the two extremes in the lives of these two characters. Can we truly call them fortunate?

Support your assertions with references drawn from **throughout** lines 616–724. All Latin words must be copied or their line numbers provided, AND they must be translated or paraphrased closely enough so that it is clear you understand the Latin. It is your responsibility to convince your reader that you are basing your conclusions on the Latin text and not merely on a general recollection of the passage. Direct your answer to the question; do not merely summarize the passage. Please write your essay on a separate piece of paper.

Scansion

Scan the following lines.

    hic nux, hic mixta est rugosis carica palmis

    prunaque et in patulis redolentia mala canistris

    et de purpureis conlectae vitibus uvae,

    candidus in medio favus est; super omnia vultus

5   accessere boni nec iners pauperque voluntas.

Vocabulary

Below you will find a list of high frequency words you have encountered in your recent readings. For all the words you know, write out full dictionary entries, including English meanings, and put a √ mark in the left-hand column to show you have already committed these words to memory. For any words you do not yet know, write out the dictionary entries using the end glossary and learn them as soon as possible.

√

1. _____ agō _____
2. _____ ars _____
3. _____ coepī _____
4. _____ crēdō _____
5. _____ dux _____
6. _____ eō _____
7. _____ flāvus _____
8. _____ flectō _____
9. _____ haereō _____
10. _____ iaceō _____
11. _____ ignārus _____
12. _____ licet _____
13. _____ lignum _____
14. _____ molliō _____
15. _____ nātus _____
16. _____ nōtus _____
17. _____ novus _____
18. _____ nox _____
19. _____ oculus _____
20. _____ ops _____
21. _____ optō _____

22. ____ *ordō* _____

23. ____ *osculum* _____

24. ____ *pateō* _____

25. ____ *pater* _____

26. ____ *pendeō* _____

27. ____ *perdō* _____

28. ____ *pēs* _____

29. ____ *sol* _____

30. ____ *tectum* _____

31. ____ *valeō* _____

32. ____ *verus* _____

33. ____ *vōs* _____

PYGMALION
METAMORPHOSES 10.238–266

"Sunt tamen obscenae Venerem Propoetides ausae
esse negare deam; pro quo sua numinis ira
240 corpora cum fama primae vulgasse feruntur,
utque pudor cessit, sanguisque induruit oris,
in rigidum parvo silicem discrimine versae.
    "Quas quia Pygmalion aevum per crimen agentis
viderat, offensus vitiis, quae plurima menti
245 femineae natura dedit, sine coniuge caelebs
vivebat thalamique diu consorte carebat.
interea niveum mira feliciter arte
sculpsit ebur formamque dedit, qua femina nasci
nulla potest, operisque sui concepit amorem.
250 virginis est verae facies, quam vivere credas,
et, si non obstet reverentia, velle moveri:
ars adeo latet arte sua. miratur et haurit
pectore Pygmalion simulati corporis ignes.
saepe manus operi temptantes admovet, an sit
255 corpus an illud ebur, nec adhuc ebur esse fatetur.
oscula dat reddique putat loquiturque tenetque
et credit tactis digitos insidere membris
et metuit, pressos veniat ne livor in artus,
et modo blanditias adhibet, modo grata puellis
260 munera fert illi conchas teretesque lapillos
et parvas volucres et flores mille colorum
liliaque pictasque pilas et ab arbore lapsas
Heliadum lacrimas; ornat quoque vestibus artus,
dat digitis gemmas, dat longa monilia collo,
265 aure leves bacae, redimicula pectore pendent:
cuncta decent; nec nuda minus formosa videtur.

Short Answer Questions

Line 239   What is the form of *negare*? _____

                  What is the use of that form? _____

                  What is the case and use of *ira*? _____

Line 240   What is the case and use of *primae*?_____

Line 243   What is the case and use of *agentis*? _____

Line 246   What is the case and use of *consorte*? _____

Line 248   What is the form of *nasci*? _____

What is the use of that form? _____

Lines 250–251   What is the form of *credas* and *obstet*? _____

What is the use of that form? _____

Line 251   What is the form of *velle*? _____

What is the use of that form? _____

Line 254   What is the case and use of *operi*? _____

Line 257   What is the form of *insidere*? _____

What is the use of that form? _____

Line 260   What is the case and use of *illi*? _____

Multiple Choice Questions *Suggested time: 12 minutes*

1. In lines 238–242, we learn that the Propoetides were turned to stone because
   a. they have dared to challenge Venus
   b. they had hearts of stone
   c. they denied the divinity of Venus
   d. they showed no sense of shame

2. The phrase *parvo . . . discrimine* (line 242) indicates
   a. that the Propoetides were nearly stone already
   b. that it took a lot to transform the Propoetides
   c. that prostitution had made the Propoetides hard hearted
   d. that people without shame are like stone

3. When the poet writes in lines 244–245 that nature gives many vices to the female mind he is guilty of
   a. litotes
   b. hyperbole
   c. irony
   d. pleonasm

4. The statement *ars adeo latet arte sua* (line 252) is best translated
   a. to such an extent does its own art lie concealed
   b. to such an extent is his art concealed by his skill
   c. his own art conceals its art.
   d. he conceals his art to a great extent.

5. In line 256 the subject of *reddi* is:
   a. Pygmalion (understood)
   b. *oscula* (line 256)
   c. *ebur* (line 255)
   d. *illud* (line 255)

6. The best translation for *tactis digitos insidere membris* (line 257) is
   a. that his fingers sunk and touched the limbs
   b. that he touched the limbs with his fingers
   c. that his fingers sunk into the limbs when he touched them
   d. that he sunk his fingers into the touched limbs

7. In line 258, *veniat* is subjunctive because it occurs in a clause that expresses
   a. a condition
   b. a fear
   c. an indirect question
   d. purpose

8. In line 264, the figure of speech employed is
   a. alliteration
   b. anaphora
   c. personification
   d. onomatopoeia

9. In line 266, *nec nuda minus formosa videtur* means
   a. that the ivory statue is just as beautiful unclothed
   b. that the ivory statue is more beautiful unclothed
   c. that the ivory statue is less beautiful unclothed
   d. that the beautiful ivory statue is not unclothed

10. In line 266, *cuncta* refers to
    a. the statue
    b. the garlands
    c. the jewels
    d. his gifts

Translation *Suggested time: 20 minutes*

Translate the passage below as literally as possible.

> "Sunt tamen obscenae Venerem Propoetides ausae
> esse negare deam; pro quo sua numinis ira
> corpora cum fama primae vulgasse feruntur,
> utque pudor cessit, sanguisque induruit oris,
> 5   in rigidum parvo silicem discrimine versae.
>
> "Quas quia Pygmalion aevum per crimen agentis
> viderat, offensus vitiis, quae plurima menti
> femineae natura dedit, sine coniuge caelebs
> vivebat thalamique diu consorte carebat.

Short Analysis Questions

1. Why is the transformation of the Propoetides into stone (line 242) appropriate?

   _____
   _____
   _____
   _____

2. What conclusion did Pygmalion draw from the crimes of the Propoetides?

   _____
   _____

3. a. Translate *virginis est verae facies, quam vivere credas* (line 250).

   _____
   _____

   b. What is the effect of the poet's second person singular use of *credas*?

   _____
   _____
   _____
   _____

4. Give five examples in English of how Pygmalion treated his statue as if it were a real woman even before he gave it gifts.

   a. _____
   b. _____
   c. _____
   d. _____
   e. _____

PYGMALION
METAMORPHOSES 10.267–297

      conlocat hanc stratis concha Sidonide tinctis
      adpellatque tori sociam adclinataque colla
      mollibus in plumis, tamquam sensura, reponit.
270   "Festa dies Veneris tota celeberrima Cypro
      venerat, et pandis inductae cornibus aurum
      conciderant ictae nivea cervice iuvencae,
      turaque fumabant, cum munere functus ad aras
      constitit et timide 'si, di, dare cuncta potestis,
275   sit coniunx, opto,' non ausus 'eburnea virgo'
      dicere Pygmalion 'similis mea' dixit 'eburnae.'
      sensit, ut ipsa suis aderat Venus aurea festis,
      vota quid illa velint et, amici numinis omen,
      flamma ter accensa est apicemque per aera duxit.
280   ut rediit, simulacra suae petit ille puellae
      incumbensque toro dedit oscula: visa tepere est;
      admovet os iterum, manibus quoque pectora temptat:
      temptatum mollescit ebur positoque rigore
      subsidit digitis ceditque, ut Hymettia sole
285   cera remollescit tractataque pollice multas
      flectitur in facies ipsoque fit utilis usu.
      dum stupet et dubie gaudet fallique veretur,
      rursus amans rursusque manu sua vota retractat.
      corpus erat! saliunt temptatae pollice venae.
290   tum vero Paphius plenissima concipit heros
      verba, quibus Veneri grates agat, oraque tandem
      ore suo non falsa premit dataque oscula virgo
      sensit et erubuit timidumque ad lumina lumen
      attollens pariter cum caelo vidit amantem.
295   coniugio, quod fecit, adest dea, iamque coactis
      cornibus in plenum noviens lunaribus orbem
      illa Paphon genuit, de qua tenet insula nomen."

Short Answer Questions

Line 267   What is the case and use of *concha*? _____

Line 269   What is the the form of *sensura*? _____

                  What does *sensura* modify? _____

                  Translate *sensura*. _____

Line 274   What is the case and use of *di*? _____

Line 278   What is the form of *velint*? _____

What is the use of that form? _____

Line 281   What is the form of *incumbens*? _____

What does *incumbens* modify? _____

Line 283   How is the form *posito rigore* used? _____

Translate *posito rigore*. _____

Line 286   What is the case and use of *usu*? _____

Line 289   What is the form of *temptatae*? _____

What word does it modify? _____

Line 291   What is the case and use of *quibus*? _____

What is the antecedent of *quibus*? _____

Lines 295–296   How is the form of the two words *coactis . . . lunaribus* used? _____

Translate *coactis lunaribus*. _____

Multiple Choice Questions *Suggested time: 12 minutes*

1. In line 267, *stratis . . . tinctis* is an ablative of
   a. means
   b. comparison
   c. place where
   d. manner

2. In lines 275–276, Pygmalion prays for a wife who is
   a. as perfect as his ivory maiden
   b. better than his ivory maiden
   c. like his ivory maiden
   d. unlike his ivory maiden

3. Line 279 (*flamma . . . duxit*) is best translated as
   a. three times the flame burnt up and the flame tip leapt up through the air
   b. three times the flame was lifted and led its tip through the air
   c. three times he lifted the flame, and led its tip through the air
   d. he lifted the flame into the air three times

4. Lines 280–281 form a
   a. chiasmus
   b. tricolon crescendo
   c. synchesis
   d. zeugma

122 • OVID

5. The poet illustrates Pygmalion's confusion in line 287 by employing a(n)
   a. oxymoron
   b. hyperbaton
   c. polysyndeton
   d. irony

6. Pygmalion in line 289
   a. leaps with delight
   b. takes the statue's pulse
   c. is tempted
   d. touches the body

7. The statue blushes in line 293 because
   a. she is naked
   b. Pygmalion kisses her
   c. she is afraid
   d. Pygmalion's kisses are false

8. The goddess attends the wedding in line 295 because
   a. she performed a miracle
   b. it is held at her city
   c. Pygmalion believes in her and her powers
   d. the statue is her child

9. In line 297 *illa* refers to
   a. Venus
   b. a child
   c. Pygmalion's wife
   d. the statue

10. Line 297 (*illa . . . nomen*) is best translated
    a. she gave birth to Paphos, a child from whom the island takes its name
    b. she gave birth to Paphos, a boy from whom the island takes its name
    c. she gave birth to Paphos, a girl from whom the island takes its name
    d. she who gave her name to the island, gave birth to Paphos

Translation *Suggested time: 15 minutes*

Translate the passage below as literally as possible.

> "Festa dies Veneris tota celeberrima Cypro
> venerat, et pandis inductae cornibus aurum
> conciderant ictae nivea cervice iuvencae,
> turaque fumabant, cum munere functus ad aras
> 5 constitit et timide 'si, di, dare cuncta potestis,
> sit coniunx, opto,' non ausus 'eburnea virgo'
> dicere Pygmalion 'similis mea' dixit 'eburnae.'

_____

_____

_____

_____

_____

_____

_____

_____

_____

Short Analysis Questions

1. What are the central ritual events at the annual festival for Venus at Cyprus as described in lines 270–273?

    a. _____

    b. _____

    c. _____

2. What is the significance of the incident described in line 279?

    _____

    _____

3. a. Translate *ut Hymettia sole/ cera remollescit tractataque pollice multas/ flectitur in facies ipsoque fit utilis usu* (lines 284–286).

b. Explain two parallels that show why this simile is particularly appropriate to describe the statue coming to life. Cite the Latin for your examples.

1.

2.

Essay *Suggested time: 20 minutes*

In the story of Pygmalion, the poet offers an antithesis between the transformations of the Propoetides and the statue. What is this antithesis and how is it developed in the passage? Write an essay in which you discuss how and why the two transformations are contrasted.

Support your assertions with references drawn from **throughout** lines 238–297. All Latin words must be copied or their line numbers provided, AND they must be translated or paraphrased closely enough so that it is clear you understand the Latin. It is your responsibility to convince your reader that you are basing your conclusions on the Latin text and not merely on a general recollection of the passage. Direct your answer to the question; do not merely summarize the passage. Please write your essay on a separate piece of paper.

Scansion

Scan the following lines.

et, si non obstet reverentia, velle moveri:

ars adeo latet arte sua. miratur et haurit

pectore Pygmalion simulati corporis ignes.

saepe manus operi temptantes admovet, an sit

Vocabulary

1. Make a list of all the gifts that Pygmalion offered to his ivory statue. Beside each Latin word provide line references in parentheses. Give the dictionary entry and meaning for each noun.

   a. _____
   b. _____
   c. _____
   d. _____
   e. _____
   f. _____
   g. _____
   h. _____
   i. _____

2. Make a list of all the verbs that describe touching or feeling. Give the dictionary entry and meaning for each verb. Cite each verb only once. Provide line references in parentheses beside each verb.

   a. _____
   b. _____
   c. _____
   d. _____
   e. _____
   f. _____

3. Make a list of all the parts of the body found in the passage. Beside each Latin word provide line references in parentheses. Give the dictionary entry and meaning for each noun..

   a. _____
   b. _____
   c. _____
   d. _____
   e. _____
   f. _____
   g. _____
   h. _____
   i. _____
   j. _____
   k. _____
   l. _____
   m. _____
   n. _____
   o. _____
   p. _____
   q. _____
   r. _____

APPENDICES
A AND B

APPENDIX A
PRACTICE EXAM 1

Question 1 *Suggested time: 20 minutes*

carmine nomen habent exterrita cornibus Io
    et quam fluminea lusit adulter ave
quaeque super pontum simulato vecta iuvenco
    virginea tenuit cornua vara manu.

Amores 1.3.21–24

    ardet in abducta Briseide magnus Achilles
        (dum licet, Argeas frangite, Troes, opes);
    Hector ab Andromaches complexibus ibat ad arma,
        et galeam capiti quae daret, uxor erat;
5   summa ducum, Atrides visa Priameide fertur
        Maenadis effusis obstipuisse comis.
    Mars quoque deprensus fabrilia vincula sensit:
        notior in caelo fabula nulla fuit.

Amores 1.9.33–40

In each of the passages above, Ovid uses lists of mythological characters to support an argument that he is trying to make. Write an essay in which you examine each of the passages and compare how successfully his mythological examples support his argument.

Support your assertions with references drawn from **throughout** both passages. All Latin words must be copied or their line numbers provided, AND they must be translated or paraphrased closely enough so that it is clear you understand the Latin. It is your responsibility to convince your reader that you are basing your conclusions on the Latin text and not merely on a general recollection of the passage. Direct your answer to the question; do not merely summarize the passage. Please write your essay on a separate piece of paper.

Question 2 *Suggested time: 15 minutes*

Translate the passage below as literally as possible.

> quis nisi vel miles vel amans et frigora noctis
>   et denso mixtas perferet imbre nives?
> mittitur infestos alter speculator in hostes,
>   in rivale oculos alter, ut hoste, tenet.
> 5   ille graves urbes, hic durae limen amica
>   obsidet; hic portas frangit, at ille fores.

Amores 1.9.15–20

Question 3 *Suggested time: 15 minutes*

>   Plura locuturum timido Peneia cursu
>   fugit cumque ipso verba inperfecta reliquit,
>   tum quoque visa decens; nudabant corpora venti,
>   obviaque adversas vibrabant flamina vestes,
> 5   et levis inpulsos retro dabat aura capillos,
>   auctaque forma fuga est. sed enim non sustinet ultra
>   perdere blanditias iuvenis deus, utque monebat
>   ipse Amor, admisso sequitur vestigia passu.
>
>   *Metamorphoses* 1.525–532

1. Discuss the significance of the word order of line 4.

2. a. Translate *auctaque forma fuga est* (line 6).

   b. Citing the Latin and translating your choices, list the three ways in lines 3–6 that the action in *auctaque forma fuga est* (line 6) is accomplished.

   3. In line 1, to whom does *locuturum* refer?

PRACTICE EXAM 2

Question 1 *Suggested time: 20 minutes*

    omnia possideat, non possidet aera Minos."
    dixit et ignotas animum dimittit in artes
    naturamque novat. nam ponit in ordine pennas
    a minima coeptas, longam breviore sequenti,
5   ut clivo crevisse putes: sic rustica quondam
    fistula disparibus paulatim surgit avenis;
    tum lino medias et ceris alligat imas
    atque ita conpositas parvo curvamine flectit,
    ut veras imitetur aves.

                                                          Metamorphoses 8.187–195

    interea niveum mira feliciter arte
    sculpsit ebur formamque dedit, qua femina nasci
    nulla potest, operisque sui concepit amorem.
    virginis est verae facies, quam vivere credas,
5   et, si non obstet reverentia, velle moveri:
    ars adeo latet arte sua.

                                                          Metamorphoses 10.247–252

In the above two passages, Ovid describes two artists and their work. In an essay, consider the craft of the artist, the purpose for which the work of art is created, and the outcome of the artist's production.

Support your assertions with references drawn from **throughout** both passages. All Latin words must be copied or their line numbers provided, AND they must be translated or paraphrased closely enough so that it is clear you understand the Latin. It is your responsibility to convince your reader that you are basing your conclusions on the Latin text and not merely on a general recollection of the passage. Direct your answer to the question; do not merely summarize the passage. Please write your essay on a separate piece of paper.

Question 2 *Suggested time: 15 minutes*

Translate the passage below as literally as possible:

> fissus erat tenui rima, quam duxerat olim,
> cum fieret, paries domui communis utrique.
> id vitium nulli per saecula longa notatum—
> quid non sentit amor?—primi vidistis amantes
> 5 et vocis fecistis iter, tutaeque per illud
> murmure blanditiae minimo transire solebant.
>
> *Metamorphoses* 4.65–70

Question 3 *Suggested time: 15 minutes*

> Mantua Vergilio gaudet, Verona Catullo;
>   Paelignae dicar gloria gentis ego,
> quam sua libertas ad honesta coegerat arma,
>   cum timuit socias anxia Roma manus.
> 5 atque aliquis spectans hospes Sulmonis aquosi
>   moenia, quae campi iugera pauca tenent,
> "quae tantum" dicet "potuistis ferre poetam,
>   quantulacumque estis, vos ego magna voco."

Amores 3.15.7–14

1. a. Cite the Latin in which the poet elevates himself to the status of Catullus and Vergil.

   b. Write out a translation for the Latin you cited.

2. a. Write out the Latin that expresses a chiasmus in line 4.

   b. What effect does this chiasmus have on the meaning of the line?

3. In lines 6–8, the poet draws a comparison between great and small.

   a. Write out the Latin that expresses each of these and translate the words.

   great: _____ _____

   small: _____ _____

   b. What is the purpose of this comparison?

PRACTICE EXAM 3

Question 1 *Suggested time: 20 minutes*

> Colligere incertos et in ordine ponere crines
>   docta neque ancillas inter habenda Nape
> inque ministeriis furtivae cognita noctis
>   utilis et dandis ingeniosa notis,
> 5   saepe venire ad me dubitantem hortata Corinnam,
>   saepe laboranti fida reperta mihi,
> accipe et ad dominam peraratas mane tabellas
>   perfer et obstantes sedula pelle moras.
> nec silicum venae nec durum in pectore ferrum
> 10   nec tibi simplicitas ordine maior adest;
> credibile est et te sensisse Cupidinis arcus:
>   in me militiae signa tuere tuae.
>
>   *Amores* 1.11.1–12

> Flete meos casus: tristes rediere tabellae;
>   infelix hodie littera posse negat.
> omina sunt aliquid: modo cum discedere vellet,
>   ad limen digitos restitit icta Nape.
> 5   missa foras iterum limen transire memento
>   cautius atque alte sobria ferre pedem.
>
>   *Amores* 1.12.1–6

In the above two passages, Ovid refers to Corinna's maid Nape. Write an essay in which you examine the characterizations that the poet develops in these two passages. How does the poet create two distinctly different Napes?

Support your assertions with references drawn from **throughout** both passages. All Latin words must be copied or their line numbers provided, AND they must be translated or paraphrased closely enough so that it is clear you understand the Latin. It is your responsibility to convince your reader that you are basing your conclusions on the Latin text and not merely on a general recollection of the passage. Direct your answer to the question; do not merely summarize the passage. Please write your essay on a separate piece of paper.

Question 2 *Suggested time: 15 minutes*

Translate the passage below as literally as possible.

> questus eram, pharetra cum protinus ille soluta
>   legit in exitium spicula facta meum
> lunavitque genu sinuosum fortiter arcum
>   "quod" que "canas, vates, accipe" dixit "opus."
> 5   me miserum! certas habuit puer ille sagittas.
>   uror, et in vacuo pectore regnat Amor.

Amores 1.1.21–26

136 • OVID

Question 3 *Suggested time: 15 minutes*

```
       talia tum placido Saturnius edidit ore:
       'dicite, iuste senex et femina coniuge iusto
       digna, quid optetis.' cum Baucide pauca locutus
       iudicium superis aperit commune Philemon:
   5   'esse sacerdotes delubraque vestra tueri
       poscimus, et quoniam concordes egimus annos,
       auferat hora duos eadem, nec coniugis umquam
       busta meae videam, neu sim tumulandus ab illa.'
```
Metamorphoses 8.703–710

1. In the above passage Philemon makes three requests of the gods. Write out and translate the Latin for each request.

   a. _____

   _____

   b. _____

   _____

   c. _____

   _____

2. a. In line 1, to whom does *Saturnius* refer? _____

   b. What is the effect of this patronymic? _____

   _____

   _____

3. Write out the Latin for and explain the metonymy in line 4.

   _____

   _____

   _____

   _____

APPENDIX B
HIGH-FREQUENCY WORD LIST

The following list contains words which occur **five** or more times in the Ovid AP passages.

ā, ab (+ abl.) from
accipiō, -ere, -cēpī, -ceptum to receive, accept
ad (+ acc.) to, at; by the light of
aes, aeris (n.) money, pay
āiō to say, assert; reply
alter . . . alter the one . . . the other
amans, -ntis (m., f.) lover
amō, -āre, -āvī, -ātum to love; to fall in love
amor, -ōris (m.) love, love affair
aqua, -ae (f.) water, sea
arbor, -oris (f.) tree
arma, -ōrum (n. pl.) arms, weapons; fighting, war
ars, -tis (f.) skill, art
at (conj.) at least, but, yet; while, whereas
atque (conj.) and in fact, and what is more, and indeed, and even
aura, -ae (f.) breeze, air
aut (conj.) or
aut . . . aut either . . . or
bellum, -ī (n.) war
carmen, -minis (n.) poetry, song
cēra, -ae (f.) wax, beeswax
certus, -a, -um accurate, precise, sure
color, -ōris (m.) color
corpus, -oris (n.) body
cum (conj.) when; (prep. + abl.) with, along with
deus, -ī (m.) god, deity
dīcō, -ere, dixī, dictum to say; to appoint, fix
digitus, -ī (m.) finger; toe
dō, dare, dedī, datum to give; to allow; to cause to go

dum (conj.) while
dux, -cis (m.) general, leader
ē, ex (+ abl.) from
ebur, -oris (n.) ivory
ego I
eō, īre, i(v)ī, itum to go
et (conj.) and; also; even
et . . . et both . . . and; also
faciō, -ere, fēcī, factum to make, do; bring about, inspire; to act; to reveal; to see that
fallō, -ere, fefellī, falsum to deceive, trick; to fail; to while away, beguile
ferō, ferre, tulī, lātum to tell, relate; to carry, bear, bring
ferus, -a, -um fierce, wild
fugiō, -ere, -ī, -itum to flee
habeō, -ēre, -uī, -itum to have, possess; to hold
hic, haec, hoc this, the latter
hostis, -is (m.) enemy
iaceō, -ēre, -uī, -tum to lie down, lie; to be overthrown
iam (adv.) now
ignis, -is (m.) fire, star
ille, illa, illud that, the former; he, she
in (+ acc.) over, affecting; for, towards; into; among; (+ abl.) in, on
inquam, inquit to say
ipse, -a, -um oneself, itself
lacertus, -ī (m.) upper arm
legō, -ere, lēgī, lectum to choose, select, pick out; to read
locus, -ī (m.) place; open land

longus, -a, -um long, tall
loquor, -quī, -cūtus to speak
magnus, -a, -um great, large
manus, -ūs (f.) hand; armed force, band
medius, -a, -um middle, middle of; between; in half, half; medium, moderate
meus, -a, -um my
mīles, -itis (m.) soldier
miser, -era, -erum wretched, miserable
modo (adv.) just now, recently, lately; just, only
multus, -a, -um much
nātus, -ī (m.) son
nec and . . . not; not even
nimium (adv.) excessively, extremely, very much
nōmen, -minis (n.) name, family name, fame, reputation
nōn (adv.) not
noster, -tra, -trum our
novus, -a, -um new, unfamiliar
nox, -ctis (f.) night
nūdus, -a, -um bare, pure, open, simple; naked, unclothed
nullus, -a, -um no one, nobody, nothing; no; insignificant, trifling
oculus, -ī (m.) eye
omnis, -e each, every, all
opus, -eris (n.) task, under taking, work, job; need
ordō, -dinis (m.) order; class, rank; a linear arrangement
ōs, ōris (n.) face; mouth
osculum, -ī (n.) mouth, lips; kiss
pārens, -entis (m., f.) ancestor, parent
pater, -tris (m.) father
pectus, -oris (n.) chest, breast
penna, -ae (f.) wing, feather
per (+ acc.) through, throughout
perdō, -ere, -idī, -itum to waste one's effort or time; to destroy
pēs, pedis (m.) foot, metrical foot
petō, -ere, -īvī, -ītum to seek, look for; to seek the hand of in marriage, to court
placeō, -ēre, -uī, -itum (+ dat.) to be pleasing or acceptable
pōnō, -ere, posuī, positum to put, place, arrange; to lay aside, abandon

possum, posse, potuī to be able
puella, -ae (f.) girl, young woman
puer, -ī (m.) boy
quī, quae, quod who, which
quis, quid who? what?
quoque (adv.) also, too
rāmus, -ī (m.) branch
relinquō, -ere, -liquī, -lictum to leave behind
saepe (adv.) often
sed (conj.) but
semper (adv.) always
sentiō, -īre, sensī, sensum to feel, sense
sī (conj.) if
sīc (adv.) thus, in this way, in like manner
sub (+ abl.) under, underneath; at the base of; (+ acc.) at the base of, just at
sum, esse, fuī, futūrus to be
suus, -a, -um his, her, its, their
tabella, -ae (f.) writing tablet
tamen (adv.) nevertheless
tangō, -ere, tetigī, tactum to touch, come in contact with
temptō, -āre, -āvī, -ātum to try, attempt; to handle, touch, feel
teneō, -ēre, -uī, -tum to hold, have; to catch
timidus, -a, -um fearful, apprehensive, timid
tōtus, -a, -um the whole of
tū you (sing.)
tuus, -a, -um your (sing.)
unda, -ae (f.) body of flowing water, river; water
ūnus, -a, -um one; alone
ut (conj.) just as, like; when; in order that; since
vacuus, -a, -um empty, unattached, free, unoccupied
vel (conj.) either . . . or; at any rate
veniō, -īre, vēnī, ventum to come
verbum, -ī (n.) word
vestis, -is (f.) clothing; cloth
virgō, -inis (f.) maiden
volō, velle, voluī to wish for; to wish
vōs you (pl.)
vulnus, -eris (n.) wound, injury

A COMPLETE VOCABULARY

Words marked with a ~ are also listed in the High-Frequency Word List.

A

ā (interj.) ah!
~ā, ab (+ abl.) from
abditus, -a, -um hidden, concealed
abdūco, -dūcere, -dūxi, -ductum to carry off
abeō, -īre, -iī, -itum to change, be transformed into
absum, -esse, āfuī, āfutūrus to be missing; to be away from
absūmō, -ere, -sumpsī, -sumptum to use up, squander, spend
ac (conj.) and
accēdō, -ere, -cessī, -cessum to follow in accordance; to be added
accendo, -ere, -di, -censum to light, ignite; (pass.) to flare up
accingō, -ere, -cinxī, -cinctum to gird, equip
~accipiō, -ere, -cēpī, -ceptum to receive, accept
accommodō, -āre, -āvī, -ātum to fasten on, fit
acer, -eris (n.) maple wood
ācer, ācris, ācre vigorous, energetic
Achillēs, -is (m.) Achilles, Greek hero of the Trojan War
acūtus, -a, -um pointed, sharp
~ad (+ acc.) to, at; by the light of
adclīnō, -āre, -āvī, -ātum to lean or rest on
adcumbō, -ere, -cubuī, -cubitum to recline at table
addūco, -ere, -dūxi, -ductum to pull taut
adeō, -īre, -iī, -itum to approach
adeō (adv.) especially, extremely, to such a degree
adflō, -āre, -āvī, -ātum to breathe onto, blow onto
adhibeō, -ēre, -uī, -itum to apply
adhūc (adv.) already; yet, as yet, still
adimō, -ere, -ēmī, -emptum to take away
adiuvō, -āre, -iūvī, -iūtum to help, assist
admittō, -ere, -mīsī, -missum to give loose rein to, release, let go
admoveō, -ēre, -mōvi, -mōtum to move or place near to
adnuō, -ere, -uī, -ūtum to nod; to nod in approval
adoleō, -ēre, -uī, adultum to burn
adoperiō, -īre, -uī, -tum to cover over
adpellō, -āre, -āvī, -ātum to call, address, name
adserō, -ere, -uī, -tum to lay claim to
adspergō, -ginis (f.) sprinkling, splashing, scattering
adspiciō, -ere, -spexī, -spectum to observe, behold, catch sight of
adsum, -esse, -fui, -fūturus to be present
adulter, -erī (m.) adulterer
adūrō, -ere, -ussī, -ustum to burn, scorch
adversus, -a, -um opposing, obstructing, standing in the way
aedēs, -is (f.) temple, sanctuary
aemula, -ae (f.) a female imitator
aēnum, -ī (n.) a pot or cauldron made of bronze
aequō, -āre, -āvī, -ātum to make level
aequor, -oris (n.) calm, flat surface of the sea
aequus, -a, -um like, equal; **ex aequo** -equally
āēr, āeris (m.) air
~aes, aeris (n.) money, pay
aestuō, -āre, -āvī, -ātum to seethe; to blaze
aetās, -ātis (f.) age
aethēr, -eris (m.) air, sky
aevum, -ī (n.) lifetime, experience, years of age
affectō, -āre, -āvī, -ātum to aspire to, attempt
agilis, -e active, busy
agitō, -āre, -āvī, -ātum to shake, brandish
agmen, -minis (n.) army
agna, -ae (f.) ewe lamb

agō, -ere, ēgī, actum to lead, drive; to deliver, give; spend (time) **quid agam** how am I?

~**āiō** to say, assert, reply

āla, -ae (f.) wing

albus, -a, -um white, clear, colorless

āles, -itis (m.) large bird

aliquis, aliquid someone, something

aliter (adv.) otherwise, differently

alligō, -āre, -āvī, -ātum to tie, fasten

altē (adv.) at a great height

~**alter . . . alter** the one . . . the other

altus, -a, -um high; deep

alumnus, -ī (m.) a "son" in the sense of a product of a particular environment

alveus, -ī (m.) a hollowed-out vessel, dish

~**amans, -ntis** (m., f.) lover

Amathusius, -a, -um of or pertaining to a town on Cyprus, sacred to Venus

ambiguum, -ī (n.) uncertainty, doubt

ambitiōsus, -a, -um vain, ambitious, conceited

ambō, -ae, -ō both, the two

amīca, -ae (f.) mistress

amictus, -ūs (m.) cloak

amīcus, -a, -um friendly, loving

~**amō, -āre, -āvī, -ātum** to love, fall in love

~**amor, -ōris** (m.) love, love affair

amplector, -ī, -plexus to embrace

an (conj.) or, or rather; whether

an . . . an whether . . . or

ancilla, -ae (f.) female slave

Andromachē, -ēs (f.) Andromache, wife of Hector

anhēlitus, -ūs (m.) gasp, panting

anīlis, -e of or pertaining to an old woman

anima, -ae (f.) soul, life; breath

animal, -ālis (n.) animal

animus, -ī (m.) courage, spirit, morale; mind, soul

annus, -ī (m.) year

ansa, -ae (f.) a handle

anser, -eris (m.) goose

ante (adv.) previously, once; in front, ahead; (prep. + acc.) before, in front of

antrum, -ī (n.) cave

anus, -ūs (f.) an old woman

anxius, -a, -um anxious, worried, troubled

Āonius, -a, -um of Aonia, Boeotian; of or connected with the Muses, poetic

aperiō, -īre, -uī, -tum to reveal, disclose

apex, apicis (m.) a tip of a flame

apis, -is (f.) bee

Apollineus, -a, -um of or pertaining to Apollo

aptō, -āre, -āvī, -ātum to fit, put into position

aptus, -a, -um (+ dat.) appropriate, fitting, suited

~**aqua, -ae** (f.) water, sea

aquila, -ae (f.) eagle

aquōsus, -a, -um watery, wet

āra, -ae (f.) altar

arātor, -ōris (m.) ploughman

aratrum, -ī (n.) plow

~**arbor, -oris** (f.) tree

arboreus, -a, -um of or pertaining to trees, arboreal

arcus, -ūs (m.) bow

ardeō, -ēre, arsī, arsum to burn, be inflamed

arduum, -ī (n.) high elevation

arduus, -a, -um tall, lofty

ārea, -ae (f.) open space out-of-doors

argentum, -ī (n.) silver

argēus, -a, -um Greek

āridus, -a, -um dry

arista, -ae (f.) harvest

~**arma, -ōrum** (n. pl.) arms, weapons; fighting, war

armātus, -a, -um armed

armentum, -ī (n.) herd

~**ars, -tis** (f.) skill, art

artus, -ūs (m.) limb of a tree or body; a joint of the body

arvum, -ī (n.) field, ploughed land; territory, country

arx, -cis (f.) summit, peak

asper, -era, -erum wild, rough, harsh

aspiciō, -ere, -spexī, -spectum to look at, gaze upon, observe

~**at** (conj.) at least, but, yet; while, whereas

āter, ātra, ātrum black, dark-colored, stained

atlantiadēs, -ae (m.) Mercury, a grandson of Atlas

~**atque** (conj.) and in fact, and what is more, and indeed, and even

Atrīdēs, -ae (m.) a male descendant of Atreus, king of Argos and Mycenae; usually used of Agamemnon

attenuō, -āre, -āvī, -ātum to enfeeble, lessen, weaken
Atticus, -ī (m.) Atticus
attollō, -ere to lift up, raise
attonitus, -a, -um dazed, astounded
auctor, -ōris (m.) founder, author, originator
auctus, -a, -um increased in intensity
audax, -ācis bold, confident
audeō, -ēre, ausus to go so far as to, dare, have the courage
audiō, -īre, -īvī, -ītum to hear
auferō, -ferre, abstulī, ablātum to carry away, carry off
augeō, -ēre, auxī, auctum to increase, augment, strengthen
Augustus, -ī (m.) Caesar Augustus, emperor
Augustus, -a, -um of or pertaining to the emperor Augustus
~aura, -ae (f.) breeze, air
aurātus, -a, -um golden
aureus, -a, -um golden
auris, -is (f.) ear
Aurōra, -ae (f.) Aurora, goddess of the dawn
aurum, -ī (n.) gold
auspicium, -ī (n.) portent, fortune, luck
~aut (conj) or
aut . . . aut either . . . or
autumnālis, -e autumnal
avārus, -a, -um greedy, avaricious, miserly
avēna, -ae (f.) stem, stalk
āversor, -ārī, -ātus to turn away from in disgust, reject
avis, avis (f.) bird
āvius, -a, -um distant, remote

B

Babylōnius, -a, -um Babylonian
bāca, -ae (f.) olive; pearl
baculum, -ī (n.) walking stick, staff
Baucis, -idis (f.) Baucis, wife of Philemon
~bellum, -ī (n.) war
bellus, -a, -um pretty, beautiful
bene (adv.) well
bicolor, -ōris having two colors

bicornis, -e having two prongs
blanditia, -ae (f.) flattery, compliment, endearing comment
blandus, -a, -um charming, seductive, carressing
bonus, -a, -um good, worthy, reliable
Boōtēs, -ae (m.) Bootes, a constellation
bōs, bovis (m., f.) bull, cow
brācchium, -ī (n.) arm
brevis, -e short
Brīsēis, -idos (f.) Briseis, Achilles' slave and concubine
būbō, -ōnis (m.) the horned owl
bustum, -ī (n.) tomb
buxus, -ī (f.) boxwood

C

cacūmen, -cūminis (n.) the tip or top of a tree
cadō, -ere, cecidī, cāsum to fall down
cādūcifer, -erī (m.) Mercury, the bearer of the caduceus
caedēs, -is (f.) slaughter, killing
caedō, -ere, cecīdī, caesum to kill, murder, slaughter
caelebs, -libis unmarried male, bachelor
caelicola, -ae (m., f.) an inhabitant of heaven
caelō, -āre, -āvī, -ātum to engrave, emboss
caelum, -ī (n.) sky, heaven
caeruleus, -a, -um blue, greenish blue
caleō, -ēre, -uī to be hot or warm
callidus, -a, -um clever, resourceful
Calymnē, -ēs (f.) an island off the coast of Asia Minor
campus, -ī (m.) field
candidus, -a, -um glistening
canis, canis (m.) dog, hound
canistrum, -ī (n.) a basket
canna, -ae (f.) a small reed
canō, -ere, cecinī, cantum to sing, tell of, relate
cantō, -āre, -āvī, -ātum to sing, celebrate in song
capillus, -ī (m.) hair
capiō, -ere, cēpī, captum to capture, contain
Capitōlium, -ī (n.) the Capitoline Hill
captīvus, -a, -um captured, hunted
captō, -āre, -āvī, -ātum to seek out; try to catch

captus, -a, -um captured
caput, -itis (n.) head
cardō, -inis (m.) hinge
careō, -ēre, -uī, -itum (+ abl.) to be lacking
cāricus, -a, -um carian, a type of fig
cariōsus, -a, -um decayed, withered
~carmen, -minis (n.) poetry, song
carnifex, -ficis (m.) executioner
carpō, -ere, -sī, -tum to pass over, pursue one's way
cārus, -a, -um beloved, dear
casa, -ae (f.) cottage
castra, -ōrum (n. pl.) camp
cāsus, -ūs (m.) misfortune, event
caterva, -ae (f.) band, squadron, troop
Catullus, -ī (m.) Catullus
causa, -ae (f.) cause, reason, inspiration
causor, -ārī, -ātus to plead as an excuse or reason
cautus, -a, -um cautious
cavus, -a, -um hollow, concave
cēdō, -ere, cessī, cessum to yield, give way; to be inferior
celeber, -bris, -bre crowded, populous, festive
celer, -eris, -ere swift
celsus, -a, -um high, lofty
~cēra, -ae (f.) wax, beeswax
Cerēs, -eris (f.) Ceres, goddess of open fields and agriculture
certē (adv.) at any rate, at least; certainly, without a doubt
~certus, -a, -um accurate, precise, sure
cerva, -ae (f.) deer
cervix, -īcis (f.) neck
cēterus, -a, -um the rest of, remaining
cicūta, -ae (f.) poisonous hemlock (*conium maculatum*)
cingō, -ere, cinxī, cinctum to gird, encircle, surround, bind
cinis, -eris (m.) ashes, embers
circumdō, -are, -edī, -atum (+ abl.) to surround, encircle
cithara, -ae (f.) lyre
citus, -a, -um rapid, speedy
clāmō, -āre, -āvī, -ātum to shout
Claros, -ī (f.) Claros, a small town, sacred to Apollo, on the central coast of Asia Minor
clārus, -a, -um loud, shrill

claudō, -ere, -sī, -sum to close, shut
clāvus, -ī (m.) nail
clīvus, -ī (m.) slope, incline
coactus, -a, -um curdled
coctilis, -e of baked bricks
coeō, -īre, -iī, -itum to come together, unite
coepī, coepisse, coeptum to begin
coerceō, -ēre, -uī, -itum to restrain, restrict, control, bind up
cognitor, -ōris (m.) attorney
cognitus, -a, -um known to be
cognōscō, -ere, -nōvī, -nitum to recognize
cōgō, -ere, coēgī, coactum to force, compel; to bring together
colligō, -ere, -lēgī, -lectum to gather together, collect
collis, -is (m.) hill, mountain
collum, -ī (n.) neck
colō, -ere, -uī, cultum to till, cultivate; to worship
~color, -ōris (m.) color
columba, -ae (f.) dove
columna, -ae (f.) column, pillar
coma, -ae (f.) hair
comes, -itis (m., f.) companion
comitō, -āre, -āvī, -ātum to follow
commendō, -āre, -āvī, -ātum to recommend, make agreeable or attractive
committō, -ere, -mīsī, -missum to entrust
commūnis, -e shared, common
cōmō, -ere, -psī, -ptum to adorn, arrange
complector, -i, -plexus to embrace
complexus, -ūs (m.) embrace
compōnō, -ere, -posuī, -positum to compose, put together
comprimō, -ere, -pressī, -pressum to pack closely or densely, squeeze
comptus, -a, -um adorned
concha, -ae (f.) shell
concidō, -ere, -ī to fall, collapse
concipiō, -ere, -cēpī, -ceptum to produce, form; to conceive
concordō, -āre, -āvī, -ātum to agree, harmonize
concors, -cordis agreeing, harmonious
concutiō, -ere, -cussī, -cussum to shake
conditus, -a, -um preserved

condō, -ere, -idī, -itum to inter, lay to rest
confugiō, -ere, -fūgī to flee to for safety
congestus, -a, -um piled up
coniugium, -ī (n.) marriage
coniunx, -iugis (f.) wife, bride; husband
conligō, -ere, -lēgī, -lectum to gather together, collect
conlocō, -āre, -āvī, -ātum to place, position, arrange
conpescō, -ere, -uī to quench
conplector, -ī, -plexus to embrace
conpōnō, -ere, -posuī, -positum to place together
conprendō, -ere, -dī, -sum to seize, catch hold of
conscius, -ī (m.) accomplice, conspirator
consenescō, -ere, -senuī to grow old
consors, -rtis (f.) partner
conspiciō, -ere, -spexī, -spectum to see, witness
constō, -āre, -stitī to take up a position; to stand up
consuescō, -ere, -suēvī, -suētum to be in the habit of, become accustomed to
consūmō, -ere, -psī, -ptum to consume, devour
contentus, -a, -um content, satisfied
conterminus, -a, -um nearby, adjacent
contiguus, -a, -um adjacent, neighboring
contingō, -ere, -tigī, -tactum to come about, happen
continuō (adv.) forthwith, immediately, without delay
contrā (+ acc.) on the opposite side; (adv.) to the opposite side
cōnūbium, -ī (n.) the rite of marriage
conveniens, -entis (+ dat.) fitting, appropriate, consistent
conveniō, -īre, -vēnī, -ventum to be suitable or adapted for; to come together, meet
convincō, -ere, -vīcī, -victum to prove, demonstrate
Corinna, -ae (f.) Corinna
corniger, -era, -erum having horns
cornū, -ūs (n.) horn, bow
cornum, -ī (n.) a cornelian cherry
~corpus, -oris (n.) body
Corsicus, -a, -um of or belonging to the island of Corsica off the western coast of Italy
cortex, -icis (m.) outer bark of a tree
crātēr, -ēris (m.) a mixing bowl for wine
crēdibilis, -e capable of being believed, credible, likely

crēdō, -ere, -idī, -itum to believe, trust
crescō, -ere, crēvī, crētum to grow, increase; arise
Crētē, -ēs (f.) the island of Crete
crīmen, -minis (n.) reproach, blame; evil thing
crīnis, crīnis (m.) hair, tresses
cruentō, -āre, -āvī, -ātum to stain with blood
cruentus, -a, -um bloody
cruor, -ōris (m.) blood; bloodshed; gore
crūs, crūris (n.) lower leg, shin
crux, crucis (f.) wooden frame or cross on which criminals were hanged or impaled
cultus, -a, -um refined, sophisticated, elegant, revered
~cum (conj.) when; (prep. + abl.) with, along with
cunctus, -a, -um all; every
cupīdō, -dinis (f.) desire, longing
Cupīdō, -dinis (m.) Cupid
cupiō, -ere, -īvī, -ītum to desire
cur (adv.) why?
cūra, -ae (f.) care, anxiety, worry; object of concern, beloved person
cūrō, -āre, -āvī, -ātum to bother with, care about
currō, -ere, cucurrī, cursum to run, fly quickly
cursus, -ūs (m.) running, rushing
curvāmen, -minis (n.) curvature, arc
cuspis, -pidis (f.) spear, lance; sharp point, tip
custōdia, -ae (f.) defence, guard
custōs, -ōdis (m., f.) watchman, doorkeeper
Cyprus, -ī (f.) the island of Cyprus
Cytherēa, -ae (f.) Venus

D

Daedalus, -ī (m.) Daedalus, builder of the labyrinth in Crete and father of Icarus
damnōsus, -a, -um ruinous, destructive,
Daphnē, -ēs (f.) Daphne, daughter of the river god Peneus; loved by Apollo and changed into a laurel tree
daps, dapis (f.) feast, meal
dē (+ abl.) from
dea, -ae (f.) goddess
debeō, -ēre, -uī, -itum to owe, be indebted to
decens, -entis graceful, attractive
decet, -ēre, -uit to be right, fitting, proper; to be becoming or appropriate

decor, -ōris (m.) beauty, good looks
dēdecet, -ēre, -uit to disgrace, dishonor
dēdicō, -āre, -āvī, -ātum to dedicate
dēferō, -ferre, -tulī, -lātum to bring down, carry down
dēfleō, -ēre, -ēvī, -ētum to lament, feel sorrow
dēlicia, -ae (f.) pleasure, delight
Dēlius, -iī (m.) Apollo
Dēlos, -ī (f.) Delos, an island in the Aegean
Delphicus, -a, -um of or connected to Delphi
dēlūbrum, -ī (n.) temple, shrine
dēmissus, -a, -um low, close to the ground
dēmittō, -ere, -mīsī, -missum to thrust, drive
dēmō, -ere, -psī, -ptum to remove, take away
densus, -a, -um thick, dense
dēpōnō, -ere, -posuī, -positum to lay aside, get rid of; to allay
dēprendō, -ere, -ī, -prensum to catch, discover
dēserō, -ere, -uī, -tum to withdraw, desert, abandon
dēserviō, -īre to serve zealously, devote oneself
dēsīdia, -ae (f.) idleness, inactivity, leisure
dēsidiōsus, -a, -um idle, lazy
dēsinō, -ere, -si(v)ī, -situm to cease, stop, desist
dēsultor, -ōris (m.) a circus rider who leaps from horse to horse
~deus, -ī (m.) god, deity
dēvoveō, -ēre, -vōvī, -vōtum to curse
dexter, -tra, -trum right, righthand
Diāna, -ae (f.) Diana, twin sister to Apollo, virgin goddess of woodlands
~dīcō, -ere, dixī, dictum to say; to appoint, fix
diēs, -ēī (f.) day
difficilis, -e troublesome
~digitus, -ī (m.) finger; toe
dignus, -a, -um worthy
dīmittō, -ere, -mīsī, -missum to direct oneself to; to let go
dīmoveō, -ēre, -mōvī, -mōtum to move about
dīrus, -a, -um dreadful, awful
discēdō, -ere, -cessī, -cessum to depart, go away
discinctus, -a, -um easygoing, undisciplined
discrīmen, -inis (n.) difference, distinction
dispār, -ris unequal, dissimilar
diū (adv.) for a long time

dīvellō, -ere, -vulsī, -vulsum to tear apart, tear open, tear in two
dīversus, -a, -um differing, distinct
~dō, dare, dedī, datum to give; to allow, cause to go
doctus, -a, -um expert, skilled
dolens, -entis grieving, sorrowing
dolor, -ōris (m.) pain, grief
domina, -ae (f.) mistress
dominus, -ī (m.) master, owner
domō, -āre, -āvī, -ātum to boil soft
domus, -ī (f.) house, home, household
dōnec (conj.) as long as
dōnō, -āre, -āvī, -ātum to give as a gift, grant
dubitō, -āre, -āvī, -ātum to hesitate; to doubt
dubius, -a, -um uncertain
dūcō, -ere, dūxī, ductum to lead; to shape, develop, mold
~dum (conj.) while
duo, -ae, -o two
duplex, -plicis twofold, deceitful, duplicitous
duplicō, -āre, -āvī, -ātum to double in size or amount
dūrus, -a, -um stubborn, hard; unsympathetic, uncaring, dull
~dux, -cis (m.) general, leader

E

~ē, ex (+ abl.) from
~ebur, -oris (n.) ivory
eburneus, -a, -um of ivory
eburnus, -a, -um of ivory
ecce (interj.) behold! look!
ēdō, -ere, -idī, -itum to publish; produce, put forth; to deliver a message, utter
efficiō, -ere, -fēcī, -fectum to cause to be, become
effūsus, -a, -um loose, flowing
~ego I
ēgredior, -ī, -gressus to go out, leave
ei (interj.) oh!
ēiaculor, -ārī, -ātus to shoot forth
elegī, -ōrum (m. pl.) elegiac verses
ēlīdō, -ere, -līsī, -līsum to expel, force out, drive out
ēlūdō, -ere, -lūsī, -lūsum to elude, avoid capture
ēmicō, -āre, -āvī, -ātum to spurt, shoot forth

ēmodulor, -ārī, -ātum to sing in rhythm
enim (conj.) indeed, truly
ensis, -is (m.) sword
~eō, īre, i(v)ī, itum to go
eōdem (adv.) to the same place
ephēmeris, -idos (f.) a record book, daybook, diary
epulae, -ārum (f. pl.) feast, banquet
eques, -itis (m.) a member of the equestrian order
equidem (adv.) truly, indeed
equus, -ī (m.) horse
ergo (adv.) therefore, for that reason
ērigō, -ere, -rexī, -rectum to raise oneself
ēripiō, -ere, -ripuī, -reptum to snatch, pluck
errō, -āre, -āvī, -ātum to wander about
ērubescō, -ere, -buī to blush with shame or modesty
ērudiō, -īre, -īvī, -ītum to teach, instruct
~et (conj.) and; also; even
et . . . et both . . . and
etiam (adv.) even; likewise; indeed
etsī (conj.) even if, although
Eurus, -ī (m.) Eurus, the east wind
exaudiō, -īre, -īvī, -ītum to hear, listen
excēdō, -ere, -cessī, -cessum to go away, pass out of, depart
excipiō, -ere, -cēpī, -ceptum to accept, receive
exeō, -īre, -iī, -itum to go out; emerge
exhorreō, -ēre to shudder
exiguus, -a, -um small, slight
exilium, -ī (n.) exile
eximō, -ere, -ēmī, -emptum to take away, banish
exitium, -ī (n.) destruction, ruin
exōsus, -a, -um hating, despising
expallescō, -ere, -paluī to turn pale
experiens, -ntis active
expers, -pertis (+ gen.) lacking experience or knowledge, free from
extendō, -ere, -dī, -tum to stretch out, thrust out
exterō, -ere, -trīvī, -trītum to wear down, trample on
exterreō, -ēre, -uī, -itum to terrify, frighten
extinguō, -ere, -tinxī, -tinctum to die, perish
extrēmus, -a -um farthest, outermost
exuviae, -ārum (f. pl.) spoils

F

fabricō, -āre, -āvī, -ātum to work, fashion, shape
fabrīlis, -e of or belonging to a metalworker, skilled; fabricated
fābula, -ae (f.) gossip, scandal, myth, story
faciēs, -iēī (f.) appearance, looks, shape; beauty
~faciō, -ere, fēcī, factum to make, do; to bring about, inspire; to act; to reveal, to see that
faex, -cis (f.) the dregs or sediment of any liquid, particularly of wine; brine
fāgineus, -a, -um of the beech tree
fāgus, -ī (f.) beech tree
~fallō, -ere, fefellī, falsum to deceive, trick; to fail; to while away, beguile
falsus, -a, -um false, not genuine
fama, -ae (f.) reputation
famulus, -ī (m.) servant, attendant
fateor, -ērī, fassus to profess, agree; acknowledge
fatīgō, -āre, -āvī, -ātum to exhaust, tire out
fātum, -ī (n.) destiny, death, end
favilla, -ae (f.) ashes of a fire
favus, -ī (m.) honeycomb
fax, facis (f.) torch, firebrand
fēcundus, -a, -um fertile, fruitful
fēlīciter (adv.) successfully
fēlix, -īcis fruitful, fertile
fēmina, -ae (f.) woman
fēmineus, -a, -um female, feminine, womanly
fera, -ae (f.) wild animal
~ferō, ferre, tulī, lātum to tell, relate; to carry, bear, bring
ferreus, -a, -um iron-like, hardhearted, unfeeling
ferrum, -ī (n.) iron, steel; blade, sword
~ferus, -a, -um fierce, wild
fervens, -ntis hot, fresh; boiling, bubbling
festum, -ī (n.) holiday, festival
festus, -a, -um (+ dies) holiday
fētus, -ūs (m.) fruit or product of a plant
fictilis, -e earthenware, pottery
fidēs, -ēī (f.) good faith, honesty, honor
fīdus, -a, -um faithful, loyal
fīgō, -ere, -xī, -xum to pierce, run through; to fix, fasten, lodge
figūra, -ae (f.) shape, appearance

fīlia, -ae (f.) daughter
fīlius, -ī (m.) son
fīlum, -ī (n.) yarn, thread
findō, -ere, fidī, fissum to split
fīniō, -īre, -īvī, -ītum to finish, end
fīnis, fīnis (m.) boundary, remotest limit
fīō, fierī to become, be made
fistula, -ae (f.) pipe, tube; pan-pipe
flāmen, -minis (n.) wind, breeze
flamma, -ae (f.) flame
flāvens, -entis yellow, golden
flāvescō, -ere to become golden
flāvus, -a, -um fair-haired, blonde; yellow
flectō, -ere, flexī, flectum to bend
fleō, -ēre, -ēvī, -ētum to weep, weep for
flētus, -ūs (m.) weeping, tears
flōs, -ōris (m.) flower, blossom
flūmen, -minis (n.) river
flūmineus, -a, -um of or associated with a river
focus, -ī (m.) hearth, fireplace
folium, -ī (n.) leaf of a plant
fons, -ntis (m.) spring of water
forāmen, -minis (n.) hole, aperture
forās (adv.) out-of-doors
foris, foris (f.) door, double door
forma, -ae (f.) appearance; good looks, beauty
formōsus, -a, -um beautiful
fors, -tis (f.) chance, luck
forte (adv.) by chance, accidentally
fortis, -e strong, courageous, brave, powerful
fortiter (adv.) vigorously, powerfully, with great force
foveō, -ēre, fōvī, fōtum to make warm
frangō, -ere, frēgī, fractum to break, smash
fretum, -ī (n.) strait, sea
frīgus, -oris (n.) cold, chill
frondeō, -ēre to grow foliage
frons, -dis (f.) foliage, leafy boughs
frons, -tis (f.) forehead, brow
fruor, -ī, -ctus to enjoy
frutex, -icis (f.) green growth
fuga, -ae (f.) flight, fleeing
fugax, -ācis running away, fleeing
~fugiō, -ere, -ī, -itum to flee

fugō, -āre, -āvī, -ātum to cause to flee, drive away, repel
fulgeō, -ēre, fulsī to glisten, gleam
fulica, -ae (f.) waterfowl, coot
fūmō, -āre, -āvī, -ātum to give off smoke
funēbris, -e deadly, funereal
fungor, -ī, functus to perform, observe
furca, -ae (f.) a length of wood with a forked end
furtīvus, -a, -um clandestine, secret

G

galea, -ae (f.) helmet
Gallicus, -a, -um of Gaul
garrulus, -a, -um loquacious, talkative, wordy
gaudeō, -ēre, gāvīsus to rejoice; to be pleased
gelidus, -a, -um icy cold
geminus, -a, -um double; pair of, twin
gemma, -ae (f.) jewel, gem
gena, -ae (f.) cheek
gener, -erī (m.) son-in-law
geniālis, -e creative, festive
genitor, -ōris (m.) father; ancestor
gens, -tis (f.) race, group of people
genū, -ūs (n.) knee
gerō, -ere, gessī, gestum to wage; to bear, carry
gestāmen, -minis (n.) load, burden
gestiō, -īre, -īvī to desire eagerly, want, be anxious to
gignō, -ere, genuī, genitum to give birth to
gloria, -ae (f.) glory
gradus, -ūs (m.) step
graphium, -ī (n.) stylus
grātēs, -ium (f. pl.) thanks
grātus, -a, -um welcome; pleasant, attractive
gravis, grave heavy, weighty; important; hard to capture
gravō, -āre, -āvī, -ātum to make heavy, weigh down
grex, gregis (m.) flock

H

~habeō, -ēre, -uī, -itum to have, possess; to hold
habilis, -e suitable, fit
habitābilis, -e inhabitable

habitō, -āre, -āvī, -ātum to live, dwell
hāc (adv.) on this side;
hāc fāciō to be on a side
haereō, -ēre, haesī, haesum to cling; to be brought to a standstill; to be perplexed, hesitate
harundō, -dinis (f.) reed; shaft of an arrow, arrow
haud (adv.) not
hauriō, -īre, hausī, haustum to swallow up, consume; to drink in, draw in
haustus, -ūs (m.) a drawn quantity of liquid, drink
Hector, -oris (m.) Hector, son of Priam, prince of Troy
Hēliades, -um (f. pl.) daughters of the sun god Helios
Helicē, -ēs (f.) the constellation Ursa Major
Helicōnius, -a, -um of Helicon
herba, -ae (f.) plant, herb
hērēs, -ēdis (m.) heir, successor
hērōs, -ōos (m.) hero
hesternus, -a, -um yesterday's
heu (interj.) alas
~hic, haec, hoc this, the latter
hīc (adv.) here, in this place
hinc (adv.) from this place; on this side
hodiē (adv.) today
holus, -eris (n.) vegetable (i.e., cabbage, turnip)
honestus, -a, -um honorable
honor, -ōris (m.) honor, mark of esteem, glory
hōra, -ae (f.) hour, time
horridus, -a, -um rough in manners, rude, uncouth; hairy
hortor, -ārī, -ātus to encourage
hortus, -ī (m.) garden
hospes, -itis (m.) visitor, stranger, guest; (adj.) of or pertaining to a guest
~hostis, -is (m.) enemy
hūc (adv.) here, to this place
humilis, -e humble, lowly
humus, -ī (f.) earth, ground
Hymēn (m.) the god of marriage, wedding
Hymettius, -a, -um of or pertaining to Mt. Hymettus near Athens, famous for its honey

I

~iaceō, -ēre, -uī, -tum to lie down, lie; to be overthrown
~iam (adv.) now
ibi (adv.) there, in that place
Īcarus, -ī (m.) Daedalus's son
iciō, -ere, īcī, ictum to strike, beat
ictus, -ūs (m.) blow, stroke, thrust
īdem, eadem, idem the same
ideō (adv.) for that reason
ignārus, -a, -um unaware, ignorant, unfamiliar, unknown, blind
ignāvus, -a, -um lazy, sluggish
~ignis, -is (m.) fire, star
ignōtus, -a, -um unfamiliar, unknown
īlia, -ium (n. pl.) the gut, groin
illāc (adv.) by that way
~ille, illa, illud that, the former; he, she
illīc (adv.) there, in that place
illinc (adv.) on the other side
imbellis, -e not suited to warfare, unwarlike
imber, -bris (m.) rain
imitor, -ārī, -ātus to imitate, resemble
immundus, -a, -um unclean, foul, impure
impediō, -īre, -īvī, -ītum to hinder, impede
impellō, -ere, -pulī, -pulsum to push forward, urge on
īmus, -a, -um the lowest, bottommost
~in (+ acc.) over, affecting; for, towards; into; among; (+ abl.) in, on
incertus, -a, -um disarranged, not fixed; not sure, uncertain
incola, -ae (m., f.) inhabitant
increpō, -āre, -uī, -itum to make a loud rattle, clang, noise
incubō, -āre, -uī, -itum to throw oneself upon
incumbō, -ere, -cubuī to lean over or on; to lie on
inde (adv.) therefore, and so
indignor, -ārī, -ātum to consider as unworthy or improper
indignus, -a, -um not deserving, unworthy
indūcō, -ere, -dūxī, -ductum to cover, spread on or over

indūrescō, -esere, -uī to harden, become hard
inermis, -e unarmed, defenceless
iners, -rtis lazy, feeble
infāmis, -e infamous, disgraced
infēlix, -icis unhappy, ill-fated, unlucky
inferior, -ius lower, bottom, second
infestus, -a, -um hostile
ingeniōsus, -a, -um clever
ingenium, -ī (n.) character, spirit, nature
ingrātus, -a, -um ungrateful, thankless
inhaereō, -ēre, -haesī, -haesum to stick, cling, attach, grasp
inhibeō, -ēre, -uī, -itum to restrain, check, stop
inīquus, -a, -um resentful, discontented
inlinō, -ere, -lēvī, -litum to smear, coat
inmensus, -a, -um boundless, immense, huge
inmineō, -ēre to be poised over
inmūnis, -e (+ gen.) free from, exempt
innītor, -ī, -nixus to lean on, rest on
innumerus, -a, -um countless, innumerable,
innuptus, -a, -um unmarried
inornātus, -a, -um not adorned, dishevelled, unarranged
inpār, -ris unequal
inpatiens, -ntis impatient
inpediō, -īre, -īvī, -ītum to hinder, impede
inpellō, -ere, -pulī, -pulsum to push, drive, set in motion
inperfectus, -a, -um unfinished, incomplete
inpiger, -gra, -grum quick, energetic, tireless
inpius, -a, -um impious, irreverent, undutiful
inpleō, -ēre, -ēvī, -ētum to fill up
inpōnō, -ere, -posuī, -positum to place on
inpulsus, -ūs (m.) thrust, blow
~inquam, inquit to say
inquīrō, -ere, -quisīvī, -sītus to inquire, ask
inrītō, -āre, -āvī, -ātum to provoke, arouse
insānus, -a, -um frenzied, mad, insane
insequor, -sequī, -secūtus to pursue
insīdō, -ere, -sēdī, -sessum to sink in, become embedded
insignis, -e outstanding, remarkable, distinguished
instar (n.) (+ gen.) according to, like
instruō, -ere, -xī, -ctum to instruct, equip, outfit

insula, -ae (f.) island
inter (+ acc.) among; between
intereā (adv.) meanwhile
intibum, -ī (n.) chicory or endive
intonsus, -a, -um unshorn, uncut
intrō, -āre, -āvī, -ātum to go into, enter
inūtilis, -e useless
invādō, -ere, -vāsī, -vāsum to attack, set on
inveniō, -īre, -ī, -tum to discover
inventum, -ī (n.) discovery, invention
invideō, -ēre, -vīdī, -vīsum to refuse, be unwilling
invidus, -a, -um envious, malevolent
Īō (f.) Io
~ipse, -a, -um oneself, itself
īra, -ae (f.) anger, rage, wrath
īrātus, -a, -um angry, furious
is, ea, id he, she, it; this, that
iste, -a, -ud that of yours
ita (adv.) thus, in this way
iter, -ineris (n.) journey, passage
iterum (adv.) again, another time
iubeō, -ēre, iussi, iussum to order, bid, command
iūdicium, -ī (n.) decision, pronouncement
iugālis, -e nuptial, matrimonial
iūgerum, -ī (n.) a measurement of land equal approximately to two-thirds of an acre
iugōsus, -a, -um hilly, mountainous
iungo, -ere, -xī, -ctum to join (in marriage)
Iūnōnius, -a, -um of or pertaining to Juno
Iuppiter, Iovis (m.) Jupiter
iūs, iūris (n.) authority, jurisdiction, power, right
iustus, -a, -um just, fair
iuvenālis, -e youthful
iuvenca, -ae (f.) heifer, cow
iuvencus, -ī (m.) young bull
iuvenis, -e young

L

lābor, -ī, lāpsus to slip, slide; to drip
labor, -ōris (m.) labor, toil, hardship, task
labōrō, -āre, -āvī, -ātum to be anxious, worried, distressed
lac, -ctis (n.) milk

~**lacertus, -ī** (m.) upper arm
lacrima, -ae (f.) tear
laedō, -ere, laesī, laesum to harm, injure
laetus, -a, -um joyful
laevus, -a, -um left, lefthand
laniō, -āre, -āvī, -ātum to tear, mangle
lapillus, -ī (m.) small stone, gem
lascīvus, -a, -um naughty, unrestrained, mischievous
lassō, -āre, -āvī, -ātum to tire, exhaust
lātē (adv.) over a large area, widely
latebra, -ae (f.) hiding place
lateō, -ēre, -uī to hide; to take refuge; to be concealed, lie hidden
Latius, -a, -um Roman
lātus, -a, -um broad, wide
laudō, -āre, -āvī, -ātum to praise
laurea, -ae (f.) the laurel/bay tree
laurus, -ī (f.) foliage of the laurel (bay) tree; the laurel tree
laus, -dis (f.) praise, glory
lea, -ae (f.) lioness
leaena, -ae (f.) lioness
Lebinthos, -ī (f.) an island off the east coast of Greece
lectus, -ī (m.) bed, couch
~**legō, -ere, lēgī, lectum** to choose, select, pick out; to read
leō, -ōnis (m.) lion
lepus, -oris (m.) hare
lētum, -ī (n.) death
levis, -e light, not ponderous
leviter (adv.) lightly
levō, -āre, -āvī, -ātum to lift off, remove; to relieve, support
lex, lēgis (f.) law, rule; **sine lege** in disorder, unruly
liber, -brī (m.) inner bark of a tree
lībertās, -tātis (f.) liberty
lībrō, -āre, -āvī, -ātum to level, balance
licet, -ēre, -uī, -itum it is permitted, one may; (conj.) although
lignum, -ī (n.) wood, firewood
līlium, -ī (n.) lily
līmen, -minis (n.) threshold, doorstep

līmes, -mitis (m.) path, track
līnum, -ī (n.) thread, string
liquidus, -a, -um liquid, fluid
lītoreus, -a, -um of the seashore
littera, -ae (f.) letter
līvor, -ōris (m.) bluish coloring, bruise
~**locus, -ī** (m., n. pl.) place, open land
~**longus, -a, -um** long, tall
~**loquor, -quī, -cūtus** to speak
luctus, -ūs (m.) grief, mourning
lūdō, -ere, lūsī, lūsum to trick, deceive
lūmen, -minis (n.) light, brilliance; eye
lūna, -ae (f.) moon
lūnāris, -e of or pertaining to the moon
lūnō, -āre, -āvī, -ātum to curve, bend
luō, **-ere, -ī** to pay as a penalty, amend for
lupus, -ī (m.) wolf
lustrō, -āre, -āvī, -ātum to move through or around, roam
lūsus, -ūs (m.) playing, sporting
lux, lūcis (f.) light of day; **sub luce** at dawn
Lyaeus, -ī -(m.) Bacchus
lyra, -ae (f.) lyre, lute

M

mactō, -āre, -āvī, -ātum to kill, slay, sacrifice
madefaciō, -ere, -fēcī, -factum to soak, drench
madeō, -ēre, -uī to grow wet
Maenas, -adis (f.) female worshipper of Bacchus, Bacchante, Maenad
magis (adv.) more
~**magnus, -a, -um** great, large
maior, -ius greater, larger
malum, -ī (n.) evil, wickedness
mālum, -ī (n.) an apple
malus, -a, -um wicked
mandō, -āre, -āvī, -ātum to order, command
māne (adv.) early in the day, morning
maneō, -ēre, -sī, -sum to remain, stay
Mantua, -ae (f.) the city of Mantua in the north of Italy
~**manus, -ūs** (f.) hand; armed force, band
margō, -inis (m.) margin

marītus, -ī (m.) husband
marmor, -oris (n.) marble
Mars, -tis (m.) Mars, god of war
massa, -ae (f.) heap, lump, mass
māter, -tris (f.) mother
māteria, -ae (f.) material, subject-matter
māteriēs, -iēi (f.) material, subject-matter
mātūrus, -a, -um mature, experienced
medicīna, -ae (f.) medicine
medicō, -āre, -āvī, -ātum to dye
medium, -ī (n.) a neutral or undecided state
~**medius, -a, -um** middle, middle of; between; in half, half, medium, moderate
medulla, -ae (f.) marrow
mel, mellis (n.) honey
melior, -ius better, finer, superior
melius (adv.) better, more fittingly
membrum, -ī (n.) part of the body; limb of tree or body
meminī, -isse to remember
mens, -tis (f.) mind; inclination
mensa, -ae (f.) table
menta, -ae (f.) mint
mereō, -ēre, -uī, -itum to earn
mergō, -ere, -rsī, -rsum to flood, inundate
mergus, -ī (m.) sea bird, gull
meritus, -a, -um deserving, just
mēta, -ae (f.) turning post, goal
metuō, -ere, -uī -ūtum to fear, be afraid
metus, -ūs (m.) fear
~**meus, -a, -um** my
micō, -āre, -āvī to flash, glitter, glisten
~**mīles, -itis** (m.) soldier
mīlitia, -ae (f.) military service
mīlitō, -āre, -āvī, -ātum to serve as a soldier, be a soldier
mille (n.) (indecl.) a thousand
Minerva, -ae (f.) Minerva, the goddess associated with handicrafts (particularly spinning) and war
minimus, -a, -um smallest, very small, least
ministerium, -ī (n.) duty, office, work
ministra, -ae (f.) an assistant
minium, -ī (n.) bright red dye, cinnabar
minor, -us smaller

Mīnōs, -ōis (m.) Minos, king of Crete
minuō, -ere, -uī, -ūtum to make smaller
minus (adv.) less, to a smaller degree
mīrābilis, -e wondrous, extraordinary
mīror, -ārī, -ātus to wonder at, be surprised
mīrus, -a, -um remarkable, extraordinary, wondrous
misceō, -ēre, -uī, mixtum to mix together, blend
~**miser, -era, -erum** wretched, miserable
miserābilis, -e pitiable
miserandus, -a, -um wretched, pitiable
mittō, -ere, mīsī, missum to let go, set free; send, shoot
mixtus, -a, -um mixed
moderātē (adv.) gently, in a restrained manner
modicus, -a, -um moderate in size
~**modo** (adv.) just now, recently, lately; just, only
modus, -ī (m.) measure, meter, rhythm
moenia, -ium (n. pl.) defensive walls encircling a town
mollescō, -ere to become soft
molliō, -īre, -īvī, -ītum to soften, weaken
mollis, -e gentle, smooth; soft
moneō, -ēre, -uī, -itum to advise, recommend
monīle, -is (n.) necklace
monimentum, -ī (n.) memorial
monitus, -ūs (m.) warning, advising
mons, -tis (m.) mountain, mountainous country
mora, -ae (f.) delay
morior, -ī, mortuus to die
moror, -ārī, -ātus to delay, wait; to hold back
mors, -tis (f.) death
morsus, -ūs (m.) bite
mortālis, -e mortal, human
mōrum, -ī (n.) the fruit of the mulberry tree
mōrus, -ī (f.) mulberry tree
mōs, mōris (m.) character, morals, behavior
moveō -ēre, mōvī, mōtum to move, strike; rouse
mox (adv.) soon
mucrō, -ōnis (m.) tip or point of a sword
multifidus, -a, -um split, splintered
multum (adv.) very, greatly
~**multus, -a, -um** much
mūnus, -eris (n.) gift, present; ritual duty

murmur, -is (n.) mutter, whisper
mūrus, -ī (m.) wall, city-wall
Mūsa, -ae (f.) Muse
mūtō, -āre, -āvī, -ātum to change, replace
mūtuus, -a, -um mutual, reciprocal
myrtus, -ī (f.) foliage of the myrtle tree

N

nam (conj.) for, to be sure
Napē, -ēs (f.) Nape
narrō, -āre, -āvī, -ātum to tell, relate
nascor, -ī, nātus to be born
Nāsō, -ōnis (m.) Naso, Ovid's cognomen
nāta, -ae (f.) daughter
nātālis, -e of or belonging to birth
nātūra, -ae (f.) nature, natural world
~nātus, -ī (m.) son
nē (conj.) lest, in order that...not; do not
~nec and . . . not; not even
necō, -āre, -āvī, -ātum to kill, put to death
negō, -āre, -āvī, -ātum to say not; to deny
nempe (conj.) to be sure, no doubt, certainly
nemus, -oris (n.) wood, sacred grove
nepōs, -ōtis (m., f.) grandson, granddaughter
neque (conj.) and . . . not
nēquīquam (adv.) in vain
nervus, -ī (m.) string of a musical instrument or bow
nesciō, -īre, -īvī, -ītum not to know, to be unfamiliar with; **nesciō quis** some, little, insignificant
neu (conj.) nor
nēve (conj.) and that . . . not
nex, necis (f.) death
nīdus, -ī (m.) nest
niger, -gra, -grum black, dark-colored
nimbus, -ī (m.) cloudburst, rainstorm
nimis (adv.) too much, excessively, too
~nimium (adv.) excessively, extremely, very much
nimius, -a, -um too much, too great
Ninus, -ī (m.) Ninus, king of Assyria and second husband to Semiramis
nisi (conj.) if not

nītor, -tī, -sus to strive, move with difficulty, exert oneself
nitor, -ōris (m.) brilliance, brightness, splendor, elegance
niveus, -a, -um white, snowy-white
nix, nivis (f.) snow
nocens, -ntis guilty
nocturnus, -a, -um nightly, of the night
nolō, nolle, noluī, not to want or wish
~nōmen, -minis (n.) name, family name, fame, reputation
nōminō, -āre, -avī, -ātum to name, call by name
~nōn (adv.) not
nōndum (adv.) not yet
nōs we
noscō, -ere, nōvī, nōtum to learn
~noster, -tra, -trum our
nota, -ae (f.) note, mark
nōtitia, -ae (f.) acquaintance
notō, -āre, -āvī, -ātum to mark, inscribe, scratch; to notice
nōtus, -a, -um famous, well-known
novem (indecl.) nine
noviens (adv.) nine times
novissimus, -a, -um last, final
novitās, -tātis (f.) novelty, strange phenomenon
novō, -āre, -āvī, -ātum to make or devise as new
~novus, -a, -um new, unfamiliar
~nox, -ctis (f.) night
nūdō, -āre, -āvī, -ātum to make naked, expose
~nūdus, -a, -um bare, pure, open, simple; naked, unclothed
~nullus, -a, -um no one, nobody, nothing; no; insignificant, trifling
nūmen, -minis (n.) divine power, divinity
numerus, -ī (m.) number, rhythm, measure, meter
nunc (adv.) now, at this time
nūper (adv.) recently
nūtriō, -īre, -īvī, -ītum to encourage, foster
nūtus, -ūs (m.) nod
nux, -cis (f.) nut
nympha, -ae (f.) demi-goddess spirit of nature, nymph; unmarried girl

O

oblinō, -ere, -lēvī, -litum to besmear, make dirty
obscūrus, -a, -um dim, dark
obscēnus, -a, -um polluted, foul, ill-omened
obsequor, -sequī, -secūtus to comply, gratify, humor
observō, -āre, -āvī, -ātum to watch over, guard
obsideō, -ēre, -sēdī, -sessum to occupy, beseige,
obstipēscō, -ere, -stipuī to be amazed, astonished
obstō, -āre, -stitī, -stātum to stand in the way, block the path
obstruō, -ere, -xī, -ctum to block, obstruct
obtūsus, -a, -um blunt, dull
obvius, -a, -um opposing, confronting
occupō, -āre, -āvī, -ātum to seize, occupy
ōcior, ōcius swifter, faster
~oculus, -ī (m.) eye
ōdī, odisse, ōsum to hate, dislike
odōrātus, -a, -um sweet-smelling, fragrant
offensus, -a, -um offended, displeased
officium, -ī (n.) duty
ōlim (adv.) a long time ago
ōmen, -minis (n.) omen
~omnis, -e each, every, all
onus, -eris (n.) burden
opifer, -era, -erum aid-bringing, helper
opifex, -ficis (m.) craftsman, artisan
ops, opis (f.) (sing.) aid, help, military strength; (pl.) wealth
optō, -āre, -āvī, -ātum to desire, wish for
~opus, -eris (n.) task, undertaking, work, job; need
ōrāculum, -ī (n.) oracular power, divine utterance
orbis, -is (m.) globe, world
~ordō, -dinis (m.) order; class, rank; a linear arrangement
Oriens, -ntis (m.) the East
Ōrīōn, -ōnis (m.) the constellation Orion
ornō, -āre, -āvī, -ātum to adorn, decorate, attire
ōrō, -āre, -āvī, -ātum to pray, beseech, beg
~ōs, ōris (n.) face; mouth
os, ossis (n.) bone
~osculum, -ī (n.) mouth, lips; kiss
ostendō, -ere, -tendī, -tentum to show, point out
ōtium, -ī (n.) leisure
ōvum, -ī (n.) egg

P

paciscor, -ī, pactus to agree upon
pactum, -ī (n.) agreement
Paeān, -nis (m.) Apollo, as healer; a hymn or praise addressed to Apollo
Paelignus, -a, -um of the Paelignian region in central Italy
pāgina, -ae (f.) page
pallidus, -a, -um pale, lacking color
palma, -ae (f.) fruit of the palm, a date
palūs, -ūdis (f.) swamp, floodwater
paluster, -tris, -tre marshy
pandus, -a, -um curved, bent, bowed
Paphius, -a, -um of or pertaining to the city of Paphos on Cyprus
Paphos, -ī (m.) the child of Pygmalion
pār, paris equal
parātus, -ūs (m.) preparation
parcus, -a, -um thrifty, frugal
~parens, -entis (m., f.) ancestor, parent
pāreō, -ēre, -uī, -itum to obey
pariēs, -etis (m.) wall
parilis, -e similar, like
pariter (adv.) in the same manner, likewise; at the same time, simultaneously
Parnāsus, -ī (m.) Parnasus, a mountain in Greece at the base of which is Delphi, sacred to both Apollo and the Muses
parō, -āre, -āvī, -ātum to prepare
Paros, -ī (f.) Paros, an island in the Aegean Sea
pars, -tis (f.) part, portion; side
parvus, -a, -um small
passus, -ūs (m.) pace, stride
pastor, -ōris (m.) shepherd
Patarēus, -a, -um of or related to Patara, a coastal city in southern Asia Minor with an oracle of Apollo
pateō, -ēre, -uī to be visible or revealed; to be open
~pater, -tris (m.) father
patior, -tī, passus to allow, permit
patrius, -a, -um of or pertaining to a father
patulus, -a, -um broad
paucus, -a, -um few
paulātim (adv.) little by little, by degrees
paulum (adv.) a little bit, to a small extent

pauper, -eris poor, scanty
paupertās, -tātis (f.) poverty
paveō, -ēre to be frightened
~pectus, -oris (n.) chest, breast, heart
pelagus, -ī (n.) open sea
pellō, -ere, pepulī, pulsum to fend off, drive away, repel; to strike, beat
Pelopēius, -a, -um of or pertaining to the Peloponnesian peninsula
penātēs, -ium (n. pl.) the household gods
pendeō, -ēre, pependī to hang, hang down, fall
Pēnēis, -idos descended from the river god Peneus
Pēnēius, -a, -um of or connected with the river god Peneus
penitus (adv.) thoroughly, completely
~penna, -ae (f.) wing, feather
~per (+ acc.) through, throughout
peragō, -ere, -ēgī, -actum to carry out, perform
perārō, -āre, -āvī, -ātum to plow through, inscribe
percipiō, -ere, -cēpī, -ceptum to catch hold of
percutiō, -ere, -cussī, -cussum to strike, beat
~perdō, -ere, -idī, -itum to waste one's effort or time; to destroy
peremō, -ere, -ī, -ptum to kill
perennis, -e lasting, enduring
perferō, -ferre, -tulī, -lātum to suffer, endure, undergo; carry, convey
perīclum see **periculum**
perīculum, -ī (n.) danger
perlegō, -ere, -lēgī, -lectum to read over, read through
permātūrescō, -ere, -tūruī to become fully ripe
perōdī, -disse, -sum to despise, loathe
perpetuus, -a, -um eternal, everlasting
persequor, -sequī, -secūtus to follow all the way, accompany
perveniō, -īre, -vēnī, -ventum to penetrate, extend, reach; to arrive
pervigilō, -āre, -āvī, -ātum to keep watch all night
~pēs, pedis (m.) foot; metrical foot
pestifer, -era, -erum deadly, pernicious, pestilential
~petō, -ere, -īvī, -ītum to seek, look for; to seek the hand of in marriage, to court
pharetra, -ae (f.) quiver
pharetrātus, -a, -um wearing a quiver

Philēmōn, -onis (m.) Philemon, husband of Baucis
Phoebē, -ēs (f.) Diana, twin sister to Apollo
Phoebus, -ī (m.) Apollo
Phrygia, -ae (f.) Phrygia, a region in central Asia Minor
pictus, -a, -um painted
Pīerides, -um (f. pl.) the Muses, daughters of Pierus
piger, -gra, -grum sluggish, inactive
pīla, -ae (f.) ball, sphere
piscis, -is (m.) fish
Pittheus, -eī (m.) Pittheus, son of Pelops and grandfather to Theseus
pius, -a, -um dutiful, conscientious, pious
~placeō, -ēre, -uī, -itum (+ dat.) to be pleasing or acceptable
placidus, -a, -um agreeable, kindly
plangor, -ōris (m.) beating, lamentation
plēnus, -a, -um full
plūma, -ae (f.) feather
plumbum, -ī (n.) lead
plūrimus, -a, -um most plentifully supplied, greatest in amount
plūs, plūris (n.) more
plūs (adv.) more
pōculum, -ī (n.) a drinking cup
poena, -ae (f.) penalty, punishment
poēta, -ae (m.) poet
pollex, -icis (m.) thumb
pompa, -ae (f.) ceremonial procession
pōmum, -ī (n.) fruit
~pōnō, -ere, posuī, positum to put, place, arrange; to lay aside, abandon
pontus, -ī (m.) sea
porta, -ae (f.) gate, entryway
poscō, -ere, poposcī to demand, ask for insistently
possideō, -ēre, -sēdī, -sessum to control
~possum, posse, potuī to be able
post (+ acc.) after
posterus, -a, -um next, following
postis, -is (m.) door jamb, door, lintel
postquam (conj.) after, when
potens, -tis powerful, mighty, influential
potentia, -ae (f.) power, influence
praebeō -ēre, -uī, -itum to offer, provide

praeceptum, -ī (n.) teaching, piece of advice
praecipitō, -āre, -āvī, -ātum to plunge down, sink
praecordia, -ōrum (n. pl.) heart, chest, breast
praeda, -ae (f.) prey
praedor, -ārī, -ātus to take as prey, catch
praeferō, -ferre, -tulī, -lātum (+ dat.) to prefer, esteem more
praeripiō, -ere, -ripuī, -reptum to seize, snatch away
praetereō, -īre, -iī, -itum to pass by
precor, -ārī, -ātus to pray for, implore, beg, beseech
premō, -ere, -ssī, -ssum to press on, push; to cover
prex, precis (f.) prayer
Priamēis, -idos (f.) Cassandra, daughter of Priam
prīmus, -a, -um first
prior, -us first, earlier
prius (adv.) first
prō (+ abl.) on account of, because of
proavus, -ī (m.) forefather
probō, -āre, -āvī, -ātum to authorize, sanction, approve
procul (adv.) far off, at a great distance
prōdūcō, -ere, -dūxī, -ductum to bring forth, lead forth
prohibeō, -ēre, -uī, -itum to prevent; to refuse
prōiciō, -ere, -iēcī, -iectum to throw down
prōlēs, -is (f.) offspring
prōmō, -ere, -psī, -ptum to bring forth, draw forth, produce
prōnus, -a, -um lying on the face or stomach, headlong
properō, -āre, -āvī, -ātum to hasten
Prōpoetides, -um (f. pl.) young women from Cyprus
prōspiciō, -ere, -spexī, -spectum to see before one, have a view
prōsum, prōdesse, prōfuī, prōfutūrus to benefit, be helpful or useful to
prōtinus (adv.) forthwith, at once, immediately, suddenly
prōveniō, -īre, -vēnī, -ventum to come into being, arise
proximus, -a, -um next
pruīnōsus, -a, -um frosty
prūnum, -ī (n.) a plum
pudor, -ōris (m.) modesty
~puella, -ae (f.) girl, young woman
~puer, -ī (m.) boy
pulcher, -ra, -um beautiful
pullus, -a, -um dingy, sombre
pulsō, -āre, -āvī, -ātum to beat, strike repeatedly
pulvis, -eris (m.) dust
purpureus, -a, -um radiant, glowing, blushing; purple, crimson
pūrus, -a, -um pure, unsoiled
putō, -āre, -āvī, -ātum to think, consider; to imagine
Pygmaliōn, -ōnis (m.) Pygmalion, king of Cyprus
Pyramus, -ī (m.) Pyramus
Pythōn, -ōnis (m.) a serpent slain by Apollo

Q

quā (adv.) where, in which direction
quam (rel. adv.) than
quaerō, -ere, quaesīvī, -sītum to require, demand; to seek
quantō . . . tantō (adv.) by however much . . . by just so much
quantuluscumque, -acumque, -umcumque however small
quantus, -a, -um how great
quatiō, -ere, quassum to shake
-que and; **-que . . . -que** both . . . and . . .
quercus, -ūs (f.) oak tree; oak garland
queror, -rī, questus to complain
~quī, quae, quod who, which
quia (conj.) because, since
quīcumque, quaecumque, quodcumque the person who, whoever, whatever
quid (adv.) why? for what reason?
quidem (adv.) certainly, indeed, it is true
quinque five
~quis, quid who? what?
quisque, quaeque, quidque each, each one, each thing
quisquis, quidquid anyone who, whoever
quō (adv.) for that reason; in order that; by which degree, by how much
quod (conj.) because; that, the fact that
quondam (adv.) once, formerly
quoniam (conj.) since
~quoque (adv.) also, too

R

radius, -ī (m.) ray of light
rādix, -īcis (f.) root; radish
rādō, -ere, rāsī, -sum to rub clean, erase; to graze, scrape, scratch
rāmāle, -is (n.) branches, twigs
~rāmus, -ī (m.) branch
rapidus, -a, -um swift-moving
raucus, -a, -um harsh-sounding, raucous
recens, -ntis recent, fresh
recipiō, -ere, -cēpī, -ceptum to receive, make welcome
recondō, -ere, -idī, -itum to close again
reddō, -ere, -idī, -itum to deliver; to give back, return
redeō, -īre, -iī, -itum to return
redimīculum, -ī (n.) band, wreath, garland
redimiō, -īre, -iī, -ītum to wreathe, encircle
redoleō, -ēre to give off a smell, be fragrant
referō, -ferre, rettulī, relātum to bring back, bring out
rēfert, -ferre, -tulit it is of importance
refertus, -a, -um crammed full
refugiō, -ere, -fūgī to shrink from, recoil from
rēgia, -ae (f.) royal palace, court
regiō, -ōnis (f.) direction
regnō, -āre, -āvī, -ātum to reign, govern, hold sway
regnum, -ī (n.) kingdom, domain
relevō, -āre, -āvī, -ātum to relieve, ease
~relinquō, -ere, -līquī, -lictum to leave behind
remaneō, -ēre, -sī, -sum to remain, stay put
rēmigium, -ī (n.) oars, wings
remollescō, -ere to grow soft again, melt
remoror, -ārī, -ātus to linger, delay
removeō, -ēre, -mōvī, -mōtum to remove
renīdeō, -ēre to smile with pleasure, beam
renovō, -āre, -āvī, -ātum to renew
reperiō, -īre, repperī, repertum to find, discover
repertor, -ōris (m.) originator, discoverer
repetō, -ere, -īvī, -ītum to repeat
repleō, -ēre, -ēvī, -ētum to refill, replenish
repōnō, -ere, -posuī, -positum to lay to rest
repugnō, -āre, -āvī, -ātum to resist, fight against
requiēs, -ētis (f.) (**requiem**, acc.) rest, relaxation
requiēscō, -ere, -quēvī, -quētum to rest, lie at rest
requīrō, -ere, -quīsīvī, -quīsītum to ask, inquire about; to seek out, look for
rēs, -eī (f.) matter, thing
rescrībō, -ere, -scrīpsī, -scrīptum to write back in response
resecō, -āre, -secuī, -sectum to cut back, trim
resīdō, -ere, -sēdī, -sessum to fall back, subside
resistō, -ere, -stitī to halt, pause
respiciō, -ere, -spexī, -spectum to look back, look around
respondeō, -ēre, -dī, -sum to answer, reply
restō, -āre, -itī to linger, remain; to stand firm; to stop
resupīnus, -a, -um lying on one's back
resurgō, -ere, -surrexī, -surrectum to rise up again
retractō, -āre, -āvī, -ātum to handle or feel a second time
retrō (adv.) backwards
revellō, -ere, -vellī, -vulsum to remove, tear away
reverentia, -ae (f.) shyness, awe, modesty
revocō, -āre, -āvī, -ātum to summon back
Rhēsus, -ī (m.) Rhesus, a Thracian
rictus, -ūs (m.) open jaws
rīdeō, -ēre, rīsī, rīsum to laugh
rigidus, -a, -um rigid, stiff
rigor, -ōris (m.) stiffness, rigidity
riguus, -a, -um irrigated, well-watered
rīma, -ae (f.) crack
rīvalis, -is (m.) rival
rōdō, -ere, rōsī, -sum to eat away, erode
rogō, -āre, -āvī, -ātum to beg, implore
rogus, -ī (m.) funeral pyre
Rōma, -ae (f.) Rome
rostrum, -ī (n.) snout, muzzle
rota, -ae (f.) wheel
rubeō, -ēre to turn red
rubor, -ōris (m.) redness
rudis, -e crude, rough
rūgōsus, -a, -um wrinkled
rumpō, -ere, rūpī, ruptum to burst, break through
rūpēs, -is (f.) rocky cliff
rursus (adv.) in addition, besides
rūs, rūris (n.) countryside
rusticus, -a, -um rustic, crude, unrefined

S

sacer, -cra, -crum sacred, holy
sacerdōs, -ōtis (m., f.) priest, priestess
saeculum, -ī (n.) generation
~saepe (adv.) often
saepēs, -is (f.) hedge
saevus, -a, -um wild, savage, untamed
sagitta, -ae (f.) arrow
sagittifer, -era, -erum loaded with arrows, arrow-bearing
salignus, -a, -um willow wood
saliō, -īre, -uī, -tum to jump, leap
salūs, -ūtis (f.) safety
Samos, -ī (f.) an island in the eastern Mediterranean Sea
sānābilis, -e curable
sanguis, -guinis (m.) blood, bloodline
sanguinulentus, -a, -um blood red
satis (adv.) enough
Sāturnius, -a, -um of Saturn, i.e., Jupiter
scelerātus, -a, -um wicked, accursed, impious
scindō, -ere, scicidī, scissum to split, rend, tear apart
sciō, -īre, -īvī, -ītum to know
scrībō, -ere, -psī, -ptum to write
sculpō, -ere, -psī, -ptum to carve
secō, -āre, -cuī, -ctum to cut
secundus, -a, -um second
~sed (conj.) but
sedeō, -ēre, sēdī, sessum to sit
sēdēs, -is (f.) house, dwelling
sedīle -is (n.) seat
sēducō, -ere, -dūxī, -ductum to move away, draw apart
sēdulus, -a, -um attentive, persistent, zealous
segnis, -e inactive, sluggish
semel (adv.) once, a single time
Semīramis, -idis (f.) Semiramis, a Syrian queen
~semper (adv.) always
senecta, -ae (f.) old age
senectūs, -ūtis (f.) old age
senex, senis old
senīlis, -e old, aged
senior, -ius older
~sentiō, -īre, sensī, sensum to feel, sense
sentis, -is (m.) bramble, briar
sepeliō, -īre, -īvī, sepultum to bury, entomb
sepulcrum, -ī (n.) tomb, grave
sequor, -quī, -cūtus to follow; to come next in order
sera, -ae (f.) a crossbar for locking a door
sermō, -ōnis (m.) talk, conversation
serpens, -entis (f., m.) snake, serpent
serta, -ōrum (n. pl.) garlands, wreaths
sērus, -a, -um late, after the expected time
servō, -āre, -āvī, -ātum to guard; save, keep
serviō, -īre, -īvī, -ītum to be devoted or subject to; to serve
sex six
~sī (conj.) if
~sīc (adv.) thus, in this way, in like manner
siccō, -āre, -āvī, -ātum to dry, dry up
siccus, -a, -um dry
Sīdonis, -idis of or pertaining to Sidon, a town on the Phoenician coast known for its puple dyeing process
sīdus, -eris (n.) constellation, star
signum, -ī (n.) signal, sign for action; military standard
silens, -entis silent
silex, -icis (m.) hard rock or stone; flint
silva, -ae (f.) forest, woodland
similis, -e like, similar
simplicitās, -tātis (f.) lack of sophistication, frankness
simul (adv.) together, with one another; at the same time
simulācrum, -ī (n.) image, statue
simulō, -āre, -āvī, -ātum to pretend, simulate
sincērus, -a, -um unblemished
sine (+ abl.) without
sinō, -ere, sīvī, situm to permit, allow to take place
sinuōsus, -a, -um having a bowed form, curved
sistō, -ere, stetī, statum to set, set down
sitis, -is (f.) thirst
situs, -ūs (m.) neglect, disuse
sōbrius, -a, -um sober, not intoxicated
socius, -a, -um of or pertaining to a partner, kindred, companionable, fellow
sōl, sōlis (m.) sun

soleō, -ēre, -itus to be accustomed to
solitus, -a, -um usual, accustomed
solum, -ī (n.) earth, soil
sōlus, -a, -um alone, only
solūtus, -a, -um loose, unfastened, undone; weak
somnus, -ī (m.) sleep, sleepiness
sōpītus, -a, -um sleepy
sopōrō, -āre, -āvī, -ātum to put to sleep
sordidus, -a, -um grimy, dirty, unwashed
soror, -ōris (f.) sister
spargō, -ere, sparsī, sparsum to scatter, strew
spatior, -ārī, -ātus to walk about
speciēs, -iēī (f.) appearance, impression
spectō, -āre, -āvī, -ātum to look at, observe
speculātor, -ōris (m.) scout, spy
spērō, -āre, -āvī, -ātum to hope for, look forward to; to expect
spēs, -eī (f.) hope, expectation
spīculum, -ī (n.) tip, point; arrow
splendidus, -a, -um bright, shining
sponda, -ae (f.) the frame of a bed or couch
spons, -ntis (f.) will, volition
spūmō, -āre, āvī, -ātum to foam, froth
stāgnum, -ī (n.) pool
statuō, -ere, -uī, -ūtum to make up one's mind, decide
sterilis, -e futile
sternō, -ere, strāvī, strātum to strew, lay low, spread over an area, throw down
stīpes, -itis (m.) tree trunk; woody branch
stipula, -ae (f.) stubble
stīva, -ae (f.) the shaft of a plow handle
stō, stāre, stetī, stātum to stand
strāmen, -inis (n.) straw thatch
strātum, -ī (n.) coverlet, throw
strēnuus, -a, -um restless, keen
strīdō, -ere, -ī to make a high-pitched sound; to whistle, shriek, hiss
stringō, -ere, -nxī, strictum to touch lightly, graze; to unsheath
strix, -igis (f.) a screech owl
stupeō, -ēre, -uī to be amazed, stunned, dazed
~sub (+ abl.) under, underneath; at the base of; (+ acc) at the base of, just at
subditus, -a, -um situated beneath

subeō, -īre, -īvī, -itum to spread upwards; to replace
sūbiciō, -ere, -iēcī, -iectum to harness, put under the control of
subscrībō, -ere, -scrīpsī, -scrīptum to write below
subsīdō, -ere, -sēdī to give way
succintus, -a, -um having one's clothes bound up with a girdle or belt
succrescō, -ere, -ēvī to grow up as a replacement, to be supplied anew
sufferō, -ferre, sustulī, sublātum to hold up, sustain weight
suffundō, -ere, -fūdī, -fūsum to pour into, overspread; to color, redden, blush
suī himself, herself, itself, themselves
Sulmō, -ōnis (m.) Sulmo, in the province of Paelignia; the town of Ovid's birth
~sum, esse, fuī, futūrus to be
summittō, -ere, -mīsī, -missum to lower
summus, -a, -um greatest; highest
sumptus, -ūs (m.) expenditure
super (+ acc.) over
superbus, -a, -um haughty, proud, arrogant
superī, -ōrum (m. pl.) those inhabiting the heavens, the heavenly deities
superiniciō, -ere, -iniēcī, -iniectum to throw over a surface
superstes, -itis surviving after death
supersum, -esse, -fuī -futūrus to remain, be left over
supīnus, -a, -um turned palm upwards
suppleō, -ēre, -ēvī, -ētum to fill up
surgō, -ere, surrexī, surrectum to rise up
surrigō, -ere, surrexī, surrectum to rise up
surripiō, -ere, -rripuī, -rreptum to steal
sūs, suis (m., f.) pig, sow
suscitō, -āre, -āvī, -ātum to rouse, restore
suspendium, -ī (n.) hanging
suspendō, -ere, -ī, -pensum to hang, suspend
sustineō, -ēre, -uī to endure, tolerate
~suus, -a, -um his, her, its, their

T

~tabella, -ae (f.) writing tablet
tābescō, -ere, tābuī to melt gradually
tabula, -ae (f.) account book

tacitus, -a, -um silent, quiet
taeda, -ae (f.) torch made of pine wood
tālis, -e such
tam (adv.) so, so very
~**tamen** (adv.) nevertheless
tamquam (conj.) as if
tandem (adv.) at last, finally
~**tangō, -ere, tetigī, tactum** to touch, come in contact with
tantum (adv.) only, merely, just; **tantum . . . quantum** just so far . . . as
tantus, -a, -um so great, such a great
tardē (adv.) slowly
tardus, -a, -um slow-moving
tectum, -ī (n.) roof, ceiling; house
tectus, -a, -um covered with a roof, roofed
tegō, -ere, texī, tectum to cover, conceal
tellūs, -ūris (f.) land, country
telum, -ī (n.) weapon, shaft
temerārius, -a, -um reckless, thoughtless, rash
Tempē (n. pl.) (indecl.) a valley known for its pastoral beauty at the foot of Mt. Olympus
temperō, -āre, -āvī, -ātum to moderate, regulate
templum, -ī (n.) temple
~**temptō, -āre, -āvī, -ātum** to try, attempt; to handle, touch, feel
tempus, -oris (n.) time; temple of the forehead
tenebrae, -ārum (f. pl.) darkness
Tenedos, -ī (f.) an island sacred to Apollo in the Aegean Sea
~**teneō, -ēre, -uī, -tum** to have, hold, preserve; to catch
tener, -era, -erum tender, sensitive; fragile
tenuis, -e fine, thin, tender
tepeō, -ēre to be warm, tepid
tepidus, -a, -um warm
ter (adv.) three times
teres, -etis smooth, rounded
tergeō, -ēre, tersī, tersum to wipe clean
tergum, -ī (n.) back
tergus, -oris (n.) back of an animal
terra, -ae (f.) earth, ground
tertius, -a, -um third
testa, -ae (f.) a fragment of earthenware
textum, -ī (n.) woven fabric, cloth

thalamus, -ī (m.) bedroom, marriage chamber
Thisbē, -ēs (f.) Thisbe
Thrēicius, -a, -um Thracian
Thynēius, -a, -um of or pertaining to the region of Bithynia
thyrsus, -ī (m.) a wand, usually covered with vine leaves, and carried by worshippers of Bacchus
tignum, -ī (n.) timber, rafter
tilia, -ae (f.) the lime (linden) tree
timeō, -ēre, -uī to fear, be afraid
~**timidus, -a, -um** fearful, apprehensive, timid
timor, -ōris (m.) fear, dread
tingō (tinguō), -ere, -nxī, -nctum to wet, soak; to dye, stain
tollō, -ere, sustulī, sublātum to pick up; to raise up
torpor, -ōris (m.) numbness, heaviness
torus, -ī (m.) cushion, bed
tot (indecl.) so many
totiens (adv.) so often
~**tōtus, -a, -um** the whole of
tractō, -āre, -āvī, -ātum to handle, manage
trādō, -ere, -idī, -itum to deliver, hand over
trahō, -ere, traxī, tractum to drag, draw; to influence
trāiciō, -ere, -iēcī, -iectum to transfix, pierce
transeō, -īre, -īvī, -itum to cross, pass through
transitus, -ūs (m.) passage
tremebundus, -a, -um trembling, quivering
tremō, -ere, -uī to tremble
tremulus, -a, -um quivering, shaking
trepidō, -āre, -āvī, -ātum to tremble, throb, quiver
tristis, -e unfriendly, dismal, sorrowful
triumphus, -ī (m.) the procession held in Rome to honor a victorious general
trivium, -ī (n.) crossroad, meeting point of three roads
Trōs, -ōis (m.) Trojan
truncō, -āre, -āvī, -ātum to strip off foliage
truncus, -ī (m.) a trunk
~**tū** you (sing.)
tueor, -ērī, tuitus to observe, watch over, guard
tum (adv.) then, at that moment
tumidus, -a, -um swollen, swelling
tumulō, -āre, -āvī, -ātum to entomb
tumulus, -ī (m.) grave
turba, -ae (f.) crowd of followers, attendants, troop

turbō, -inis (m.) whirlwind
turpis, -e loathsome, repulsive, shameful
tūs, tūris (n.) incense
tūtēla, -ae (f.) guardian, protection
tūtus, -a, -um safe, secure
~tuus, -a, -um your (sing.)

U

ūber, -eris plentiful, abundant
ubi (adv.) where, when
ubīque (adv.) everywhere, anywhere
ullus, -a, -um any
ultimus, -a, -um final, last
ultrā (adv.) further, beyond that point
ulva, -ae (f.) rush, marsh grass
umbra, -ae (f.) shade, darkness, shadow
umbrōsus, -a, -um shady
umerus, -ī (m.) shoulder
umquam (adv.) never, ever (with *nec*)
ūnā (adv.) at the same time
~unda, -ae (f.) body of flowing water, river; water
undēnī, -ae, -a eleven at a time
ūnicus, -a, -um one, only one
~ūnus, -a, -um one; alone
urbs, -is (f.) city
urna, -ae (f.) urn
ūrō, -ere, ussī, ustum to burn, inflame with passion
usque (adv.) all the way
usus, -ūs (m.) use, purpose
~ut (conj.) just as, like; when; in order that; since
uterque, utraque, utrumque each, each . . . of the two
ūtilis, -e useful
ūtor, ūtī, ūsus (+ abl.) to make use of
ūva, -ae (f.) a bunch of grapes, grape
uxor, -ōris (f.) wife

V

vacō, -āre, -āvī, -ātum to be empty, unfilled, vacant
~vacuus, -a, -um empty, unattached, free, unoccupied
vadimōnium, -ī (n.) a legal term referring to a guarantee that the parties in a suit will appear before the court at an agreed upon date and time

vagus, -a, -um shifting, moving about
valē, valēte farewell! good-bye!
vānus, -a, -um unreliable
vārus, -a, -um bent outward
vātēs, -is (m.) poet, prophet
-ve (conj.) or
vehō, -ere, vexī, vectum to carry
~vel (conj.) either . . . or; at any rate
vēlāmen, -minis (n.) garment, veil
vellō, -ere, vulsī, -sum to pull up
vēlō, -āre, -āvī, -ātum to cover
vēlox, -ōcis swift, speedy
velut (adv.) just as, just like, in the same way that
vēna, -ae (f.) blood vessel, vein
venia, -ae (f.) justification, excuse, indulgence
~veniō, -īre, vēnī, ventum to come
venter, -tris (m.) belly
ventilō, -āre, -āvī, -ātum to fan, brandish
ventus, -ī (m.) wind
Venus, -eris (f.) Venus, goddess sacred to love and lovers
~verbum, -ī (n.) word
vērē (adv.) truly, indeed
verēcundus, -a, -um modest
vereor, -ērī, -itus to be afraid
Vergilius, -ī (m.) Vergil
vērō (adv.) truly, really
Vērōna, -ae (f.) the city Verona in the north of Italy
verrō, -ere, versum to pass over, skim, sweep; to row
versō, -āre, -āvī, -ātum to turn
versus, -ūs (m.) a line of verse or writing
vertex, -icis (m.) the top of the head
vertō, -ere, -tī, -sum to turn into, change
verum (conj.) but
vērus, -a, -um real, genuine
vester, -tra, -trum your (pl.)
vestīgium, -ī (n.) footprint, sole of a foot, track
~vestis, -is (f.) clothing; cloth
vetō, -āre, -uī, -itum to forbid, prohibit
vetus, -eris old, of a former time, ancient
via, -ae (f.) journey, march, way
viātor, -ōris (m.) traveller
vibrō, -āre, -āvī, -ātum to wave, flutter

vīcīnia, -ae (f.) proximity
vīcīnus, -a, -um neighboring, close by
vicis (f.) (gen.) exchange, interaction; **in vices** by turns, alternately
victrix, -īcis victorious
victrix, -īcis (f.) victorious female
videō, -ēre, vīsī, vīsum to see, observe, gaze upon; to consider
vigil, -ilis (m.) sentry, guard
vīlis, -e worthless, common, ordinary
villa, -ae (f.) rural dwelling
vincō, -ere, vīcī, victum to defeat, conquer
vinculum, -ī (n.) chain, bond
vīnum, -ī (n.) wine
violentus, -a, -um violent, aggressive
vir, -ī (m.) man, husband
vireō, -ēre, -uī to sprout, show green growth
virgineus, -a, -um of or relating to a maiden, virgin
virginitās, -tātis (f.) maidenhood
~virgō, -inis (f.) maiden
vīs, vīs (f.) (pl.) strength
viscus, -eris (n.) innermost parts of the body
vīsō, -ere, -ī to view

vīta, -ae (f.) life
vitiō, -āre, -āvī, -ātum to impair, cause defects in
vītis, -is (f.) grapevine
vitium, -ī (n.) defect, fault; vice, moral failing
vītō, -āre, -āvī, -ātum to avoid
vitta, -ae (f.) headband
vīvō, -ere, vīxī, vīctum to live
vix (adv.) hardly, scarcely
vocō, -āre, -āvī, -ātum to call
volātus, -ūs (m.) flying, flight
volō, -āre, -āvī, -ātum to fly
~volō, velle, voluī to wish for; to wish
volucris, -cris (f.) bird
voluntās, -tātis (f.) willingness, intention
~vōs you (pl.)
vōtum, -ī (n.) vow, oath, prayer
vox, vōcis (f.) voice
vulgō, āre, -āvī, -ātum to prostitute
vulgus, -ī (n.) general public, crowd, masses
~vulnus, -eris (n.) wound, injury
vultur, -uris (m.) vulture
vultus, -ūs (m.) facial expression; face

LLWS LATIN LITERATURE WORKBOOK SERIES

The volumes in this workbook series contain the Latin text that is on the AP* syllabus accompanied by exercises (grammar, translation, short answer analysis, scansion if appropriate, figures of speech, and essay questions) that will both help students to read and understand the literature as well as prepare for the AP* examination. In addition, teacher's manuals that feature the entire student text along with the answers are planned for each title.

A HORACE WORKBOOK
David J. Murphy & Ronnie Ancona

Student Text: xii + 204 pp. (2005) 8½" x 11" Paperback, ISBN 978-0-86516-574-8
Teacher's Manual: xvi + 271 pp. (2006) 6" x 9" Paperback, ISBN 978-0-86516-649-3

A VERGIL WORKBOOK
Katherine Bradley & Barbara Weiden Boyd

Student Text: xiv + 261 pp. (2006) 8½" x 11" Paperback, ISBN 978-0-86516-614-1
Teacher's Manual: xviii + 302 pp. (2007) 6" x 9" Paperback, ISBN 978-0-86516-651-6

AN OVID WORKBOOK
Chabra Adams Jestin & Phyllis B. Katz

Student Text: x + 160 pp. (2006) 8½" x 11" Paperback, ISBN 978-0-86516-625-7
Teacher's Manual: xii + 172 pp. (2007) 6" x 9" Paperback, ISBN 978-0-86516-626-4

A CATULLUS WORKBOOK
Helena Dettmer & LeaAnn A. Osburn

Student Text: xii + 244 pp. (2006) 8½" x 11" Paperback, ISBN 978-0-86516-623-3
Teacher's Manual: xvi + 328 pp. (2007) 6" x 9" Paperback, ISBN 978-0-86516-624-0

A CICERO WORKBOOK
Jane W. Crawford & Judith A. Hayes

Student Text: x + 238 pp. (2006) 8½" x 11" Paperback, ISBN 978-0-86516-643-1
Teacher's Manual: xiv + 250 pp. (2007) 6" x 9" Paperback, ISBN 978-0-86516-654-7

*AP is a registered trademark of the College Entrance Examination Board, which was not involved in the production of, and does not endorse, this product.

 **BOLCHAZY-CARDUCCI PUBLISHERS, INC.**
WWW.BOLCHAZY.COM

Ways to Enhance Latin Teaching

The Wisdom of the Ancients on
Latin Buttons

Button size: 2¼" wide

Order from our website: www.BOLCHAZY.com

Use in your oral proficiency sessions

NOTE: Buttons do not have the English translations on them.

eLitterae Newsletter

eLitterae is a monthly e-mail newsletter containing teaching tips, website specials, and other information about the Classics community.

eLitterae subscribers get breaking news, too, about the availability of new titles from Bolchazy-Carducci Publishers and access to special discounts.

To subscribe, go to: http://www.bolchazy.com/newsflash/elitterae.htm

 **Bolchazy-Carducci Publishers, Inc.**
www.BOLCHAZY.com

Ovid for College and AP*

Ovid
Amores, Metamorphoses Selections
2nd edition

Charbra Adams Jestin & Phyllis B. Katz

What is the appeal of Ovid's *Amores* and *Metamorphoses*? His *Amores* are written with wit and humor—and sometimes the regret—of one who has seen love first hand. His *Metamorphoses*, an epic story of transformations, is the work of a consummate storyteller. This book is organized to help students read, comprehend, and enjoy the voice of a poet that rings as clear at the beginning of the third millennium as it did on the eve of the first.

> Rome's wittiest poet is more and more at the center of the Latin curriculum in schools, colleges, and universities. Now what Ovid's teachers and students need more than ever are good texts and commentaries to make this sophisticated artist accessible at intermediate as well as advanced levels. This splendid edition of selected poems from Ovid's early *"Amores"* and his masterpiece the *"Metamorphoses"* will serve its intended teachers and their students very well.... This is a distinguished addition to the AP* curriculum.
>
> –James Tatum, Aaron Lawrence Professor of Classics, Dartmouth College

The Student Edition includes:
- Latin text: *Met.* I.452–567; IV 55–166; VIII.183–235; VIII.616–724; X.238–297; *Amores* I.1, I.3, I.9, I.11, I.12, III.15.
- Introduction for each passage
- Vocabulary and notes on same page as text
- Complete vocabulary in back
- Separate section of translation questions and answers on facing pages
- Glossaries of metrical terms and figures of speech
- High frequency vocabulary list
- Translation tips for reading Ovid
- Illustrations
- Maps

The Teacher's Edition includes:
- A note to the teacher
- Suggestions for teaching scansion
- Large-print text of the passages
- Translations of the passages
- Sample texts—AP* format
- Topical bibliography

Student Text:
xxviii + 196 pp.
(1999, revised reprint 2000)
6" x 9" paperback
ISBN 978-0-86516-431-4

Teacher's Editon:
viii + 72 pp.
(1999, revised reprint 2000)
8.5" x 11" paperback
ISBN 978-0-86516-496-3

*AP is a registered trademark of the College Entrance Examination Board, which was not involved in the production of, and does not endorse, this product.

 **Bolchazy-Carducci Publishers, Inc.**
www.Bolchazy.com

A Different View of the Romans

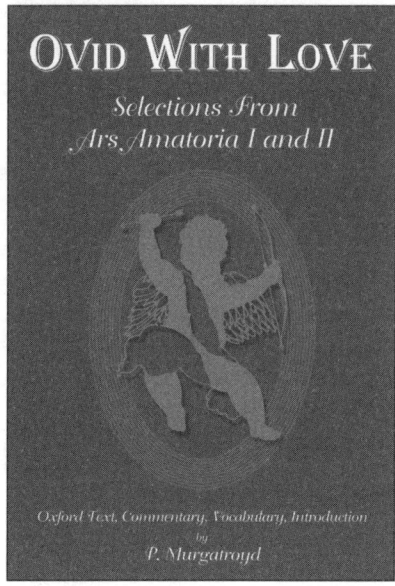

Ovid With Love
Selections from Ars Amatoria
Books I and II

Oxford Text, Commentary, Vocabulary,
Introduction by Paul Murgatroyd

Murgatroyd's *Ovid with Love* has a lot to offer the first-time reader of Ovid's *Art of Love*: masterfully selected passages from *Ars Amatoria* I and II, totaling 770 lines • textual notes that give syntactical guidance as well as insights into Ovid's style and the Roman cultural, mythological, and historical context of his poetry • a full vocabulary.

The introduction covers • Ovid's life and times • the genre of love-poetry and how the urbane and sometimes cynical Ovid and didactic *Ars* fit into it • scansion • metrical and stylistic effects • and a bibliography for further reading.

Ovid's wit, sophistication, and keen psychological insight into the foibles of humans in love cast a fresh new light on what is often misread as the thoroughly somber and serious world of the Romans. *Ars Amatoria* is a refreshing surprise for anyone well versed in Vergil, Cicero, and Caesar.

This book makes a nice introduction to Latin poetry for students coming from Latin grammar.... But irritation with the first half of the Introduction (10 pages) melts before the satifisactions of the Commentary (160 pages). Before I turn to it, let me add that the sections on scansion and on metrical and stylistic effects in the second half of the Introduction are clear and effective. Alliteration, chiasmus, anaphora, rhythmic effects, and all their brethren are described and provided with examples. The Commentary consistently points out such devices in the text, so any attentive student should begin consciously to enjoy Ovid's style.

M. knows what students will fumble over when first reading poetry. He assumes thorough knowledge of grammatical forms but provides extensive help with syntax. For instance, for the *clause arte regendus Amor* (1.4), he supplies *est* but does not say what form *regendus* is. The vocabulary does not include oblique forms (e.g., *nactae*, 1. 54, must be found under *nanciscor*). M. seldom translates a difficult line; he gives the students all the help they need too work it out for themselves.

Beyond these virtues, the notes also provide a wealth of information about Roman customs, mythological and historical allusions, literary references (especially Ovid's parody of didactic poetry). M. points out the humor in various descriptions, the point of comparisons, puns, and ambiguities. In specific contexts, he notes Ovid's psychological insight. He does splendidly what he had hoped to do: he makes the text come alive.

The selections seem well-chosen, adding up to 770 lines of text. The Introduction and Commentary are photocopied from typescript but are easy to read. The Bibliography is brief and general. The book would be fun to read with a class. I do recommend that any teacher who uses it counteract the influence of the word "trivial" and, more important, have a thorough class discussion of Ovid's use (sometimes ironic use) of sexist stereotypes!

—Eva Stehle, *NECN*

---

x + 228 pp. (1982, Reprint 1990, 2002) 6" x 9" Paperback, ISBN 978-0-86516-015-6

Bolchazy-Carducci Publishers, Inc.
www.BOLCHAZY.com

Options for Reading Ovid

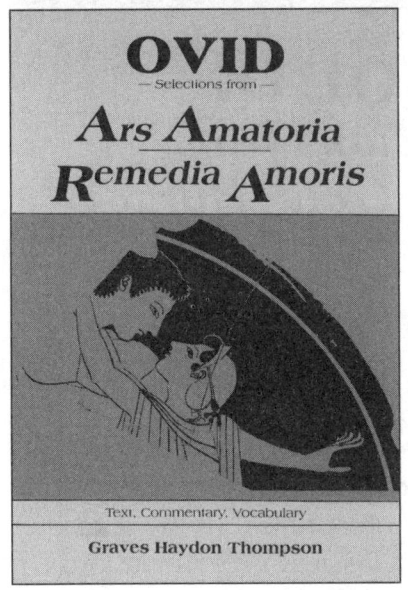

Ovid
Selections from Ars Amatoria Remedia Amoris
Text, Commentary, Vocabulary
Graves Haydon Thompson

In his *Handbook of Latin Literature* H. J. Rose states, "Didactic Poetry had already been tried often enough, and sometimes it had been mildly humorous; Ovid hit on the brilliant plan of making it amatory, and thus achieved a masterpiece, never equaled in its own kind."

Thompson has enhanced Ovid's Latin text with an excellent introduction, line-by-line notes, English summaries for the main sections and a basic vocabulary fold-out page. His well-chosen selections, copious notes and pithy summaries make this text an entertaining and effective learning tool for advanced students.

Text includes: • Introduction with chapters on Ovid's life and suggestions on reading the *Ars Amatoria* and *Remedia Amoris* • Original Latin texts (based on the 1916 Teubner edition by R. Ehwald with changes in readings, spellings, and punctuation) • Line-by-line notes • English summaries for each major section • Fold-out in back with basic vocabulary

168 pp. + foldout (1952, corrected 1958, sixteenth reprint 1977, 1997) 6" x 9" Paperback, ISBN 978-0-86516-395-9

Ovid
Metamorphoses, Book 1
A. G. Lee

This intermediate reader offers text (Book I. lines 1–779), vocabulary, and notes that are both informative and entertaining. The notes focus on fine points of grammar and rhetoric, shades of meaning, and allusions to both classical and modern literature.

viii + 162 pp. (1953, Reprint 1988) 6" x 9" Paperback, ISBN 978-0-86516-040-8

Bolchazy-Carducci Publishers, Inc.
www.BOLCHAZY.com

THE POETRY OF THE ANCIENT AUTHORS IS BEST APPRECIATED BY ORAL READING AND LISTENING

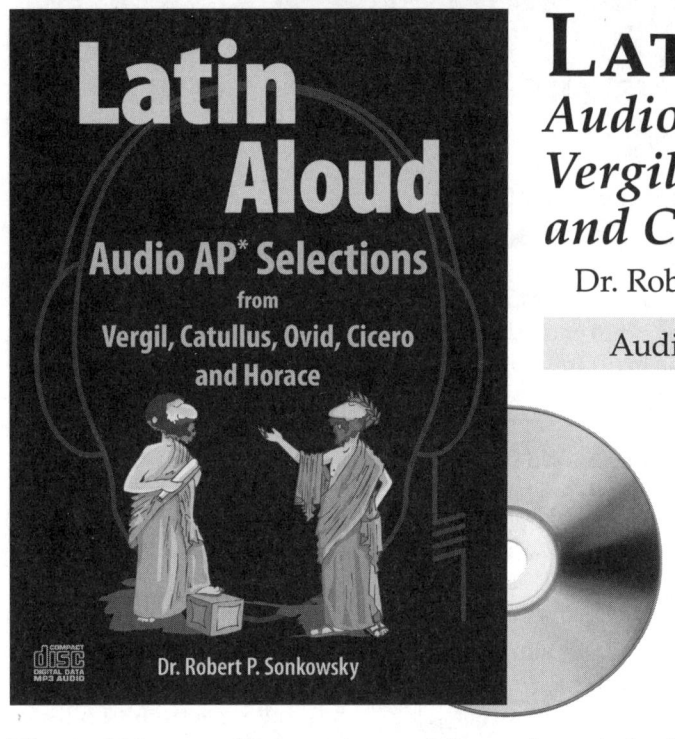

LATIN ALOUD:
Audio AP* Selections from Vergil, Catullus, Ovid, Horace and Cicero

Dr. Robert P. Sonkowsky

Audio CD (2007) MP3 files on CD UPC 00007

Latin Aloud presents 101 Latin Masterworks on CD. With a run-time of over five hours, these dramatic interpretations by a master of the Restored Classical Pronunciation, Dr. Robert P. Sonkowsky, plays on any computer and most contemporary CD and DVD players. Rip to your iPod or other MP3 player for Latin on-the-go, anytime, anywhere.

These 101 recordings, restored from the original masters and converted to MP3 for maximum availability and affordability, contain:

Vergil AP* Selections – *Aeneid, Georgics, Eclogues*
Catullus AP* Selections – 34 Poems, Including Catullus 64
Ovid AP* Selections – *Amores, Metamorphoses*
Cicero AP* Selections – *de Amicitia* and *Pro Archia* (entire)
Horace AP* Selections – 17 *Odes, Satire* 1.9

Latin Aloud affords teachers and students alike an opportunity to hear the poetry and prose of ancient authors—recited, as the writer likely intended. Researched and recorded by an authority on the Restored Classical Pronunciation of Latin, these readings improve oral proficiency and comprehension while teaching the lilt and meter of the language.

ABOUT THE NARRATOR:
Dr. Robert P. Sonkowsky is a professor emeritus of Classical and Near Eastern Studies at the University of Minnesota. He is an authority on Latin rhetoric and the pronunciation of Golden Age Latin. He has been performing the works of Latin and Greek authors for over forty years.

*AP is a registered trademark of the College Entrance Examination Board, which was not involved in the production of, and does not endorse, this product.